If He Did It For Me

By Sharon J. Thomas

Copyrights secured 2020 belonging to the author Sharon J. Thomas. Duplication without prior permission is prohibited. Printed and Bound in the United States of America. All rights reserved worldwide.

All scripture quotations, unless otherwise indicated, are taken from the *Holy Bible, King James Version (KJV). Copyright 1961. In addition to the Holy Bible, New International Version (NIV). Copyright 1973, 1978, 1984, 2011 by Biblica, Inc. Used by permission. All rights reserved worldwide.*

Forever Grateful

      I want to thank God for remembering me as He was shaping the lives of an abundance of people globally, He saw fit to include…me.

      Secondly, I would like to thank my family for giving me the space I needed to do Gods work in the vineyard, including my peculiar circle of friends like Pastor M. Singleton who started me behind his pulpit, Pastor Gooddine who helped me cultivate my gift, Pastor Allen who never doubted who I was in God, Zenobia, Valerie, Cherryann and Patricia who kept me encouraged through the storms while God stretched me for his purpose. Let me not forget my mentors Katherine and Jeffrey who helped me understand what the wilderness is while being strong in the Lord and in the power of His might (Ephesians 6:10 NIV)! You all in some way have encouraged me to water the seed that God birthed within me through the testimonials of women who felt they are all alone within their journey of life issues…I am extremely grateful that with all the billions of people in the world by His mercy and grace especially with my imperfect self He assigned me to broken women to tell their individual stories while I maintained their dignity, identity and discretion…

The Beginning

As a six-year-old child Unique never understood why other children did not like her or want to befriend her in any way, form or fashion. It was disheartening, lonely and depressing all at the same time. But she chose to remain positive and grow forward with the understanding that someday there would be a change and it was going to work out somehow.

It was a lonely road because the outside world was all she had toward any kind of happiness because for whatever reason she felt she did not fit in at home or with her other siblings; two brothers and one sister. Even then she believed in her young mind she was the one missing something and chose not to make a big deal out of it and she would better understand as she aged. She really did not understand why her father was never a part of any outings when they ventured out with mom. Nonetheless, Unique was the happiest when they traveled outside of home because her mom introduced them to other family members that she did not know existed and they had no problem excepting Unique for who she was...a member of the family who was in need of love and attention.

Conversely, when Unique's mom took her children out shopping she gave instructions like this as she gazed down upon them with an angry expression "don't ask for nothing I cannot afford it, when we go in act like you got some sense and don't touch nothing and anyone that does not follow my instructions will meet up with me when we get back home"...and they all knew what that meant. Well of course one of her brothers decided to act up and Unique's mom talked to him while she was disciplining him when they got home. Then he got a double portion from dad once he arrived from work. Some of us may remember what that was like. Ouch!

Six years later Unique's life at home became unbearable so she joined extra activities at school in efforts of avoiding the aspects of home. At the age of twelve Unique learned that life at home was very dysfunctional and scary. As years went by the dysfunction continued and it started to affect her siblings. At the age of fifteen her sister became promiscuous and at the age of sixteen and seventeen her brothers linked up with the hard-core dope dealers in the neighborhood, but Unique got more and more involved in extra school activities such as three-day trips and tutoring so she would not flunk. Unique cried herself to sleep every night as she would hear her mom begging her dad to stop and somehow through all of that she drifted to sleep after crying so hard it took the energy out of her to stay awake.

    When Unique awakened the next morning for school the house was quiet and everyone was getting ready for the day as if nothing had happened the night before as usual. Her mom was in the kitchen cooking breakfast for her and her dad, dad walked in with a cheerful "good morning" while they sat quietly at the table to eat what mom prepared. Her mom's face was caked with make-up to hide the bruises on her face. Unique began to think would she make it out of the dysfunctional atmosphere they called home. When her sister turned seventeen, she moved out of the house to go live with her nineteen old boyfriend's rented room…he was a high school dropout within six months shy of him graduating for reasons unknown, but as she thought to herself at least he had a job.

Unique's brothers were so caught up in the game visits were slim to not at all. As a matter of fact, the only time her brothers came by consistently was to give their mom some money and waved goodbye to Unique as they walked out the door. There was never a stop let me talk to my little sister moment and that hurt Unique to the core of her heart so she felt insignificant in their lives. There were times during visits Unique believed one day would be the last time she saw either one of them because of their life choices.

She started to wonder what was the purpose of having a family if they could not perform like one. She often wondered if she confided with someone at their church would the pastor relieve her father of his position as a head Deacon, would there be whispers of her being possessed as having a lying spirit or would they be exiled out of the church. Surely someone had to notice the frequent bruising on her mom's face…yet no one said or did nothing. Unique started to think if God was real why hasn't he answered her prayers for peace, unity and healing of everyone's mind within her family.

Cosandra was eight when her dad left her mom Mary without warning for another woman with no means of taking care of the household responsibilities. Her mom became a stay at home mom when she birthed Cosandra so, her skills were not up-to-date with the current market. Cosandra overheard her mom express to her best friend Antionette on the phone "*I do not know how we're going to make it*" as she sobbed overwhelmingly. Cosandra's mom took on small jobs just to make the ends meet, but did not make enough to really make it work because something was always getting disconnected. So, her mom decided to accept a night job because it paid more. Cosandra saw her mom less and less while she stayed with her mom's best friend Antionette.

It seemed as though her mom never had a day off and Cosandra started to contemplate her mom did not want her either. She started to believe that it was her fault why her parents separated in the first place. Whenever her mom did have a day off, she was always on the phone with a male friend which took away from their short time together. One late night while in her room sleeping, she was awakened to loud laughter coming from her mom's bedroom. Cosandra got really happy, jumped out of bed and rushed to the door of her mom's bedroom because she had not heard her mom laugh in a very long time. But just as she was about to knock on the door a man's voice stopped her in her tracks so she returned to her bedroom with her head hanging low in disbelief.

How could her mother do this to their only time together? Was he the reason her mom was never home anymore claiming to be at work? At the age of fifteen she wondered if he was going to eventually move in. Cosandra was preparing to ask her mom all these questions the next morning. When she got to her mom's bedroom door it was open so she cautioned herself before she entered, but there was no male in sight. So, Cosandra thought that she would ask her questions on their ride to the mall. Consequently, she thought. Cosandra awakened her mom to ask if they were still going to the mall but her mom replied *"I'm sorry baby mommy is tired and that she would make up for it on her next day off."*

Cosandra started to feel like every time she forgave her mom her mom would consistently let her down to the point, she became depressed. Her mom was so caught up with her night life that she had not noticed Cosandra was very withdrawn and she stopped asking for special quality time. Her mom did not seem to mind because she no longer suggested time with Cosandra. Cosandra started exampling this behavior at school as well, but she never explained to them why she was feeling the way she was. She just told them *"you know how we teenagers are, one day we are up and some days we are down, yet we always pull it together."* This seemed to satisfy their curiosity and they left her alone.

Later that afternoon a girl bumped into Cosandra very hard then the girl acted as if Cosandra was the one who bumped her and pushed Cosandra down. The girl was known as Lilly and she was part of a gang called *"The Sweethearts"* and this was one of their ways of initiating new recruits into their gang. After Lilly pushed Cosandra down Cosandra *forgot where and who she was. She got up clenched her fist to hit Lilly and knocked her down in the school hallway while the other students were chanting "fight, fight, fight."* By the time teachers came out of the classrooms and worked their way through the crowd to see what was going on Cosandra was on top of Lilly hitting her with fist blows to her head like nobody's business while crying and screaming "*leave me alone*!!!"

Subsequently, though the only one that ended up in the principal's office was Cosandra since an ambulance had to be called for Lilly. The principal told Cosandra she had broken Lilly's nose and the only reason why she was not going to be suspended was because the school cameras showed Lilly started it. Cosandra knew in her heart she did not mean to break Lilly's nose; it was just that she was angry about her life and felt no one wanted her. She did not know she could get so angry and she knew there would be repercussions from Lilly's friends in the gang; she just did not know when.

Not spending quality time with her mom took a toll on Cosandra and she simply stopped talking for several weeks giving into a deeper depression until her mom's best friend heard Cosandra crying in the bedroom provided for her while her mom was at work. When Antionette sat down next to Cosandra and listened to how Cosandra and her mom were not spending quality time together she just held Cosandra in her arms while telling her it was going to be alright. At this point, Antionette decided it was time to see what was going on with her friend, all the while feeling what could make her deny the love her child so urgently needed. How many of us have been in a situation that took us some place where we should not be thus hurting those closes to us? What if Antionette stopped watching Cosandra what would happen to her or should Antionette even care since she was getting married in the next couple of months? After all this was not her child.

     Johanna was a beautiful little girl at the ripen age of eight with long hair, fair skinned and very poised. Everywhere she went everyone was always telling her how beautiful she was. So, she grew up thinking her beauty would take her far in life. Her mom Hanna and her dad Joseph was always having to bring her down off her high horse so to speak in letting her know beauty was not everything and it was only skin deep. Everywhere Johanna went she was always the center of attention and when she turned twelve it did not get any better.

Now, even though Johanna recognized her own beauty she did not let it suppress her education. Johanna was on the principal list at school, class president, an active volunteer in her community and on the cheerleading squad. By the time Johanna turned fifteen the boys were relentless in trying to make her their arm piece. But her father was not having that and implemented a curfew. Of course, Johanna was upset about it because all her friends did not have a curfew at sixteen and she felt like he was treating her like a baby.

Johanna deemed since she was achieving scholar grades in school there should be a reward. Her father explained to her there were dangers out there she was not ready for and it was not her he did not trust but it was people outside their household he needed to protect her from. What her father did not know was Johanna was having her first infatuation with a boy at school named Mike. Mike had extended an invitation to her for his small group house party. Mike was very popular; an achieving scholar and he too was on the principal list. Johanna just knew if her father could just meet him the trust factor would not be an issue.

    Johanna's closest friend Veronica tried to convince her to sneak out of the house and she would make sure she got back home before her parents found out. Johanna replied *"girl is you crazy my parents would kill me"*, but her friend was very cunning by bringing up Mike's name frequently to persuade Johanna to come to the party with her so she could also have someone there she trusted to have her back. So, Johanna waited until her parents went to sleep, got in her friend's car a couple of houses down the street from her home and away they went.

    When they got to Mike's house the music was bumping and Johanna could not help but think she wished her parents was this cool to allow such a great party like this to play out at her house. As she walked in, she saw Mike making his way to the door in a perfectly white linen outfit to greet her and

Veronica disappeared into the crowd with her boyfriend. Mike greeted Johanna and said "*I was not sure if you were going to make it but I am so glad you are here.*" And she replied "*how in the world did you get your parents to agree to this*"...he said "*don't sweat it; they do not know because they are out of town but he figured they would not mind because he was a great student at school.*" This sent a shiver up Johanna's spine and she instantly felt she needed to find Veronica and go home. Then she talked herself out of it because Mike was so fine and she might not ever get another opportunity like this, so she stayed.

      Johanna began thinking this is the best night ever and she was glad she came. As her and Mike danced the night away, she began to feel dizzy, so Mike took her up to his bedroom to get a handle on what was making her dizzy. While she laid across the bed Mike offered to get her some water at which point, she did not remember what her answer was, but that he was such a gentleman. She began to think about how Mike repeatedly stated how beautiful she was and the way he said it; it felt different from everyone else. As she went in and out of consciousness, she remembers seeing Mike finally returning to the room, but he had four other guys with him she immediately recognized as being young men she had turned down their advancements for her to be their girlfriend and as she looked back at Mike she also noticed there was no water in his hand…she tried to get up but could not. She began thinking where is Veronica and did she see him bring her upstairs then passed out for a short moment.

      Stacey was tom boyish when she was nine years of age because she played often with her two older brothers. She did not find joy in doing the girly things, but took great pride in sitting in front of the television with her dad Brooklyn, oldest brother David and second oldest brother Christopher watching sports all day until dinner time. Her mom Tarron had passed away during her birth. On Mother's Day they would visit the grave where her mother was buried, but because she had no memory of her, she just watched as her three hero's sobbed as they reminisced on how they missed her. They would also release doves on her birthday at her mom's grave site.

When Stacey reached twelve years of age, she still did not find the little girl within, she continued to play around like she was a little boy. She played touch football, laser tag, basketball and raced her playmates from point A to point B. When she turned thirteen her father remarried to a woman named Sheila, her brothers moved out to find themselves as adults and she still did not know who she was. She did not like the fact that everything had changed and she only got to see her brothers during holidays or when it was time to visit her mom's grave site.

There was a change coming over Stacey that she quite did not understand like why she was having dreams of dating girls instead of boys. Although, her father always made time for her and nothing changed after he remarried, she did not feel comfortable talking to him about it and had not connected with her dad's new wife enough to talk to her; although she had every opportunity to do so. She knew she would be setting herself up for ridicule by telling anyone at school the feelings that were constantly on her mind and began to wonder what was wrong with her. She somehow knew something was not natural about the way she was feeling and wanted it to go away.

While playing basketball in the park one day with her friends she notices a young girl watching every move she made. At first, she thought the young girl was out there may be watching her boyfriend playing hoops. The girl was very pretty and seem to have it all put together. The girl did not talk or speak she just watched Stacey with precision and interest. When the game was over Stacey made her way toward her gym bag to retrieve her towel to wipe her face and arms. As she wiped down the young girl started walking toward Stacey and for some odd reason Stacey had butterflies in her stomach.

The young girl got closer and closer at which point she stopped in front of Stacey to introduce herself as Peaches. Stacey did not want to seem rude so she introduced herself. The young girl was very easy to talk to and it seemed like their conversation went on for hours. Stacey was so engulfed in their conversation she did not notice that her friends had left the park without her. So, she explained to Peaches she had to leave, and then asked where she lived. It turned out

Peaches was new to the neighborhood right around the corner from where Stacey lived.

When they got to Peaches house, Peaches leaned in and kissed Stacey then went in the house with no explanation. Although Stacey was shocked and caught off guard, she enjoyed what just happened. Stacey began to think this was her first kiss and it felt good. The fact that they were both girls at the age of thirteen did not enter into her thought process because at that moment nothing was going to take the place of how good she felt deep down inside. It no longer felt unnatural it felt right, so she thought.

Stacey found it very hard to go to sleep because she kept rehearsing what happened to her earlier that day. She started to wonder how this all came about and who could she talk to about the mixed feelings she was having about her sexuality. She did not live in a neighborhood where she saw couples of the same sex…she was more confused than ever. She just could not wrap her young mind around it as to why this was happening to her and then she finally drifted off to sleep.

The next day she went to school and anxiously wanted to run into Peaches. Then at last she had seen Peaches coming out of her economics class, they had spoken briefly and when the dismissal bell rang, they walked home from school together. The closer they got to Peaches house the more nervous Stacey became. Stacey did not know whether to lean in for another kiss or let Peaches take the lead when they reached Peaches home…she decided to lean in. However, the front door swung open to a woman's voice saying *"what do you think you're doing" get away from my daughter and then yelled at Peaches to get in the house now*!

      Stacey was both scared and devastated that she might not ever see Peaches again. So, the next day she looked for Peaches at school but was told Peaches did not come to school that day. This went on for about three weeks until one Monday Peaches appeared again coming out of her economics class. This time they cut the rest of their classes so they could be together and discussed what happened after the incident at Peaches front door. Peaches started to cry as she showcased her bruises and explained there were more but she was kept home so they could heal.

Then Peaches shared her life happenings of home life with Stacey. She told Stacey that the woman who came to the door was her stepmom who was married to her disabled dad Jim. As Peaches continued to talk, she told Stacey through a tear stained face that her stepmom has been molesting her since she was seven years old and there was no one to do anything about it because her real mom died five years after Peaches was born due to cancer. Her father Jim was so distraught from it he had a stroke and has been wheelchair bound ever since.

When it seemed like someone was going to find out or getting to close to the truth as to what was going on at her home her stepmom hired a moving company for the fourth time to pack their belongings and that's how they ended up around the corner from Stacey. Peaches also explained the stepmom has been physically abusing her every time she dared to get close to anyone. She also warned Stacey that if her stepmom find out they are still seeing each other she would probably hurt Stacey in the worse way. Without thinking about it Stacey leaned in and kissed Peaches. Little did they know Peaches stepmom Katy was watching the whole time even as they walked home.

Macaela was eight when she moved to the United States with her mother Adaego, father Idunnuola and younger brother Abdu who was six. It took several years to get to the United States because it was hard to get visa's for the entire family. Nonetheless, in 2002 the family's prayers had finally been answered and by the time Macaela turned twelve years of age her and her family were well adjusted into the Unites States. Both of Macaela's parents found work quickly at minimum wage. But Macaela and her brother however did not adjust well with school. Most of the students were mean and always picking on them because of the way they dressed (African attire) or the inability to understand their beautiful dialog when they spoke aloud. Every day while walking home from school there would always be a bunch of boys at a particular home on the steps shooting dice and sometimes it made Macaela and Abdu very nervous because sometimes during the game some of the participants became very loud and somewhat angry as they lost their money.

Macaela and Abdu's relationship with their parents were very close so each night at dinner time they would discuss the happenings of each day and before each night fell, they prayed as a family. Each morning the family got up at 5:00 am and prayed for one hour before starting their day. Macaela's brother loved to talk and he would not skip a beat each day while they walked to and from school. He always talked about what he wanted to be when he grew up and also asked many, many questions Macaela did not know what to answer first, but she managed to answer them all throughout each day as they walked home. Although Macaela loved her brother sometimes she wished he would simply be quiet.

Abdu decided to sign up for the basketball and tennis try outs at school. Abdu got into both sporting event try outs, but Abdu chose tennis because it reminded him of his life in Nigeria with his friends. Abdu was always being told by his tennis coach he had a bright future in tennis because of his ability to catch on at such an alarming rate. Coach

Joseph would work with Abdu each day on new techniques in efforts of sharping the gift that was inside of Abdu, which meant he was kept beyond school hours. Therefore, rather than just sit around waiting for Abdu to finish up every day after school Macaela decided to sign up for the chest try outs because it was the only event that ended the same time as her brothers sporting practice.

Macaela and Abdu were well on their way to making a name for themselves at school because of their after-school activities and gradually they acquired many friends through the individual school activities they separately had chosen. This gave Abdu more and more things to talk about each day to and from school. Of course Macaela wished he would simply be quiet, but that never happened and she would often think that her brother would be a great public speaker verses a tennis player; she even laughed to herself because she thought all this enduring of his talking all the time…something good has got to come out of this.

Macaela was glad when they reached home because that was the only time the talking would temporarily end because they both had hours of homework to do. Conversely, though Abdu had another opportunity to speak as their dad went around the table when he asked how everyone's day was. He would make sure Abdu went last because he always had much more to say than everyone else.

It was time to go to bed and as Macaela drifted off to sleep she reminisced on her life in Nigeria and how blessed she was besides from the friendships she developed but on how her and her family made it out of such multitudes of poverty and death. She immediately remembered one of her friends named Adaku whose mother was expecting a baby. Adaku was so excited about having a sibling that her face just lit up when she spoke about it to Macaela although her sibling would not be born for another six months. Macaela and Adaku wondered if her sibling would be a boy or a girl but it really did not matter to Adaku because she felt that news of a birth was a true blessing for any family.

Macaela did not see Adaku for two days and decided that after school she would stop by her house to make sure she was okay. Macaela was watching the clock like a hawk and at last school was over and Macaela could stop by Adaku's home. Macaela knocked on the door and as the door opened, she almost did not recognize Adaku's face because her normal glow was gone and Adaku seemed lost for words, then out of nowhere Adaku started to cry uncontrollably which made Macaela cry with her friend. So Macaela just held her friend in her arms until she was ready to talk...hours later. When she finally stopped crying Adaku uttered the words *"my sibling is dead and my mom is fighting for her life due to a large amount of blood loss."*

    At the age of eleven Macaela did not know what to say, but she knew that they needed to seek the face of God so Adaku would not lose her mom; even though the odds were against them because medical supplies and doctors were slim to none when it came to survival in Nigeria. So, Macaela asked Adaku's dad if it would be okay to invite her mom and dad to come over to offer hope as well as prayer; he said in a very low voice *"okay"*. When Macaela ran home to tell her mom and dad what had happened then stated how they were needed; her parents welcomed the opportunity to encourage their neighbors. Once they reached Adaku's home they immediately assembled everyone in the larger room and they all began to call upon Jesus the highest and the only wise God.

Before they knew it, the Holy Spirit took over, a dance erupted inside the house and they could also hear the other neighbors joining in on the praise dance outside the house. Macaela could not account how long this went on because no one cared as long as Adaku and her family received the peace and healing for the mother and wife of the house needed at their time of need. However, it astound Macaela on how many people were actually outside Adaku's home once they were leaving to go home…it seemed as though there was a telegram sent to every home in the immediate area and everyone came to the point it was a multitude of people everywhere in front of Adaku's house dancing and thanking God! When Macaela and her family reached home they had Macaela deliver two plates to Adaku and her dad. When Macaela returned they thanked God for showing up, and showing out on behalf of their neighbor before they started to eat.

Macaela had awakened to her alarm to get up for school and vaguely remembered closing her eyes once she laid down for bed the previous night after the praise dance of victory. Conversely, though once she was close to getting ready for school her mom called for her to come. When she reached the room, her mom was in she saw her friend Adaku standing before her crying again only this time she came to tell the good news that her mom was coming home! She excitedly told the story that her father told her of how the doctors gave up thus requesting Adaku's dad to call in the family members to say goodbye and how miraculously her mom's heart beat got stronger and stronger once he held his wife's hand then kissed her on the forehead! At that point, his wife opened her eyes and said "*good morning sir*" as a tear rolled down his face. He began to tell her what had transpired the night before when the neighbors came together to pray to God for her recovery.

When Adaku's mom came home within two days she explained to Adaku that she was sorry she could not hold her sibling within her because the doctors discovered that she was high risk and the next time she is with child she will be placed on complete bed rest with closely watched doctor appointments. Adaku expressed to Macaela and her mom that God not only saved her mom's life but kept her mom from being barren through the cares of the community who helped her family reach God in a very unselfish and caring way.

Immediately after the good news testimonial Macaela, Adaku and Abdu starting walking to school. Once on the way Abdu starting talking as usual, but both Macaela and Adaku did not mind they briefly looked at each other and starting giggling all the way to school. Time seemed to move very fast and Macaela was happy about that because she was still a little tired from the previous day praise event.

Upon the end of the school day an announcement came over the intercom that all after school events were canceled so both Abdu and Macaela started walking home. As they were passing the home where the young men were playing their angry men game of dice gun shots rang out, the young men starting running in several different directions all the while returning gunfire.

Macaela screamed to her brother as he was tying his shoe…sáré Abdu sáré (run)!! Macaela ran back toward her brother who fell during his escape from gunfire and when she reached him, she saw blood pouring out of his leg. She kept trying to pull her brother to safety all the while trying not to get hit by the showers of flying bullets, but he was just too heavy. It was at that moment a bullet hit Macaela and she lost consciousness as she laid beside her brother holding his hands.

The Wilderness

The behavior of Unique's family continued for several more years as Unique was about to turn seventeen she vowed to herself she was moving out when she turned eighteen years of age. Her sister returned home at the age of twenty with a two-year old baby girl named Porsha because her boyfriend decided he did not want to be a daddy. So, her sister packed her belongings and came back home to restructure a better life for her daughter at least that is what she told their mom. Unique thought to herself once she found out what was really going on at home her sister would be leaving again.

It felt awkward for Unique having her sister back in the house since her sister was last there four years ago with no contact whatsoever. Yet, it was nice to have a niece in the house who took to Unique right away and somehow whenever Porsha got up in the morning, she would make her way down the hall to Unique's room. Porsha would enter

Unique's room and plant little slobbery kisses on Unique's face before she got up.

At first, Unique thought the roof was leaking so she thought nothing else about it until she had awakened the next day with the same slobbery substance drooling down her face again. She looked up at her bedroom ceiling and saw no signs of a leak. Conversely, though one morning something startled Unique and she was too scared to move so she kept her eyes closed.

Unique thought it was her father coming into her room in error after one of his drunken events from the night before so she pretended to be asleep and without warning she felt a little slobbery substance running down her face. At which point she peeked opened one eye and saw two-year-old Porsha making her way out of her room. Unique could not help herself but shed a tear because it was at that moment, she felt significant to somebody. This became a ritual for Porsha and Unique as Unique continued to pretend every morning she was asleep just so she could receive her slobbery blessing to start her day. Unique thought to herself as she was preparing to leave for school that it took this very small being after a lifelong survival of anticipation to come into her life to confirm the implication of her love was known toward Unique and that made her eyes weld up with tears; it was her seventieth birthday.

Unique just knew when she returned home from school cake, ice cream and her family screaming "HAPPY BIRTHDAY" would be the highlight of the ending of her day. But instead she turned the key in the door and found the entire house in hysteria, blood on a towel on the floor, kitchen table turned on its side, shattered dishes and food on the floor and no one was home except her dad halfway laying across his bed with a strong smell of his favorite alcoholic beverage. She looked in every room for her mom, then she ran upstairs and down the hall looking for her sister and Porsha but there was no one to be found! Then she ran to her room where there was a note on the bed from her mom.

The note said "*Unique I am sorry for the way things turned out for your birthday, but I have left your father because after over twenty years of marriage I just cannot take it anymore. I cannot afford to take you with me, and did not want to interrupt your chance of graduating…but I do have your sister and Porsha with me to get Porsha out of harm's way. As soon as I can afford all of us, I will come get you…love mom.*" Unique was shaken to the core because not only was her mom gone, she left her behind and she took away the only joy she felt in a very long time…how was she going to survive each day now without the love of Porsha. Being caught up in the moment Unique locked her bedroom door stumbled to her window as she sobbed violently to jump, but when she stepped up on the ledge it separated from the wall and she fell back inside to the floor.

Then she heard a voice say "**come unto me and I will give you rest.**" She stopped crying and gazed around the room knowing that she locked the door behind her to execute her plan of suicide, but there was no one there so she laid down in a fetus position because she was scared. Unique ended up crying herself to sleep. When she awakened the next day, she started crying after seeing the piece of the window ledge that reminded her of the results of her attempted suicide. As time went on Unique started spiraling out of control, she started ditching her classes (six months prior to her graduation), linked up with some troubled students and started smoking marijuana. As she smoked the marijuana, she kept rehearsing the thoughts of the letter her mom left behind and how her father moved a lady friend of his into their house two weeks after her mom's escape from domestic violence. As crazy as it may have seemed her dad never laid a hand on his lady friend…ever.

Unique witnessed him pulling out her chair each time she sat at the dinner table and this is where she would always ask to be excused. One evening her father followed her to her bedroom and whispered to her "*if she did not like it there…she could leave at any time*!" Unique could not believe what she was hearing and as night fall approached, she waited for her dad and lady friend to reach his bedroom closing the door behind them, she creeped to the shed and smoked a joint. The next morning, she left for school before anyone got up and met up with her new found troubled teen friends of course returning home after school hours. Unique checked the mail, pulled a school letter addressed to her parents from the mailbox, and stuffed it in her school bag so she could read it in her bedroom.

It stated that she was being left back in the 11th grade unless she attended summer classes. Unique was so scared she did not know what to do especially if her dad found out. She knew she had to do something quick! So, before the night was over, she lied to her dad and said she was approved to work at a summer camp for kids and would be gone…and before she could get the rest of her words out, he said, "*yes*".

Her father really was not remotely interested all he heard was the word… *gone*. He did not ask for a permission slip, documentation on where she would be or any contact information. Nonetheless, and because Unique babysat from time to time she saved up her money to stay in a hotel in the next county over so she would not run into her dad going to school each day on the express public bus. Unique stopped hanging out with her troubled teen friends and stopped smoking pot so she would not be stuck living with her dad because she still did not hear from her mom or her sister, yet. But she knew she had to stay focused, brave and press toward her intended goal…freedom from feeling insignificant.

Antionette grew tired of all the questions rolling around in her head and decided to take a drive down to what she believed was where her friend Mary was working. So, she wiped the tears off of Cosandra's face and told her she was concerned about her mom so she was going to check on her. She also explained to Cosandra that mom's usually do not purposely avoid spending time with their children and something had to be wrong. She also asked Cosandra not to give up on her mom until they find out what was wrong. Cosandra looked up from her tear stained face and replied "*okay*".

As a result, they left Antionette's home with no certainty as to what they would find. As Antionette drove her car what seemed like an eternity to get to her mom's employment Cosandra could not help to think finally she was about to find out what she's been yearning to learn…what she did to deserve this and how she herself could turn back the hand of time so her mom would love her again. Cosandra had her own set of questions rolling around in her head like why did her father leave her and not so much as tried to reach out to her ever again? What was the reasoning behind her mom's behavior, and did she feel stuck in life because of Cosandra? Just as Cosandra continued to over think her situation the car stopped.

    Cosandra looked up and they were in front of a diner named "*Last Stop Café.*" Antionette took a deep breath, grabbed Cosandra's hand and they walked into the diner. Antionette decided to sit down and order a couple of ice cream sundaes and when the waitress reached their table, Antionette ordered the sundaes then she asked the waitress for Mary the waitress replied "*you're gonna have to talk to the manager,*" then called for the manager. While waiting for the manager to appear she did not see Mary anywhere in the diner. Then a voice said "*hello my name is Jack how can I help you*" then she replied "*hello my name is Antionette is Mary working tonight?*"

    Jack looked at Antionette with great confusion and then said "*Mary has not worked here in six or seven months.* Antionette was taken aback then she heard the manager say *however, if you come with me, I will give you her last known employer information that he received from one of his staff members.* Jack wrote the place of employment down as "*The Real Men's Club.*" At which point, Antionette knew her friend was in trouble because this place was known for drug use and stripping. Antionette looked over at Cosandra and how she was enjoying her ice cream sundae, then thought to herself that she should not believe the worst because her friend could very well be a bartender or waitress.

Both her and Cosandra finished their sundaes. It was then Antionette explained to Cosandra that the next place they were going to she could not go in because you have to be twenty-one and she would have to stay in the car. Antionette had parked across the street. Even though Cosandra was turning sixteen in two days Antionette knew Cosandra would be safe as well as out of any present danger if something jumped off as she went in "*The Real Men's Club.*" As Antionette made her way in she heard sensual music playing for the women who were performing on the poles while the waitress served the gentlemen their drinks.

It was dark and swarming with men which made it difficult to find Mary. At that moment she heard a distinctive but recognizable voice; it was Mary dancing for a gentleman sitting in a chair while he was engaged in every moment. She tapped Mary on the shoulder and asked her *"what do you think you are doing"*…and just as Mary turned around, she saw the man that she was dancing for; it was her fiancé. With tears streaming down her face she ran toward the door as fast as she could. Her fiancé Jeff and Mary took off after her equally stating they were sorry.

    Antionette spun around and screamed at both of them how betrayed she felt. *Mary how could you do this to me! What about Cosandra and Jeff what about us! You both lied to me repeatedly so you could be together! I extended my trust, time and to think out of concern for you Mary I watched your daughter every night!*

    She pulled off her engagement ring and threw it at her fiancé and just as she was about to go out the door…there was Cosandra standing there with a tear stained face. Before anyone could stop Cosandra she ran back out the door then without thinking Cosandra darted out into traffic and was hit by a car. Both Mary and Antionette screamed at the top of their lungs "*noooooo!!!*" When traffic stopped abruptly both Mary and Antionette also ran out into traffic as they watched Cosandra's still body bleeding profusely from her ears, nose and mouth.

Once the ambulance arrived the police cleared the street for a trauma helicopter to land. The ambulance EMT quickly asked did anyone know the victim and Mary replied while shaking "*her name is Cosandra and she's my daughter.*" He said ma'am this does not look good and judging from her injuries she is going to need surgery as well as lots of blood. In addition, we need you on the helicopter and just as Mary was about to board the helicopter she looked up and saw Antionette's outpouring of tears as their eyes locked. Mary then asked if her sister could come along for support and Antionette was ushered onto the helicopter. Cosandra was flown to the nearest trauma center for children as both Mary and Antionette sat in complete silence.

Mary and Antionette continued to sit in silence as the helicopter landed on the roof of the Children's Trauma Center. Mary was thinking how she lost the only friend that has been by her side since the abandonment of her husband and what would she do if she lost her daughter. While Antionette was thinking it was her fault because she was the one who brought Cosandra and had she not brought her she would not be fighting for her life at a trauma center. Nevertheless, they were both ushered to the waiting room with over flowing tear stained faces.

It was not long before the doctor came in requesting the attention of Cosandra's parents. He said *"Cosandra has an intracerebral hemorrhage also known as brain bleed and has a 29% to 55% survival rate. However, because of Cosandra's age she may recover quickly or she may remain in a state of impaired consciousness for an undetermined amount of time. He then stated he needed permission to repair the ruptured blood vessel and as a precaution he asked that Mary also give some blood in case Cosandra needs it while she is here in the hospital.*

Johanna awakened several times in Mike's bedroom to see a different boy taking their turn in assaulting her as she consistently screamed through a tearful uncontrollable sob

"Noooooo! Get off me! Somebody please help me!" Of course, the music was too loud for anyone to hear her pleas of anguish. All of the young men in the room with her laughed as she tried to fight back while someone was holding her legs and arms. It was very painful and she wished they would just stop and eventually they did which seemed like forever. Once they were done three of the young men left the room except Mike and one other young man who stood Johanna up against themselves to help walk her out of the bedroom and down the stairs.

Veronica was having a great time with her boyfriend and she reached toward him to give him a hug to thank him for coming. When she tilted her head upward to tip toe over his shoulders, she saw Johanna being helped down the stairs. She ran toward the bottom of the stairs and asked what's wrong with her! Mike replied *"she had too much to drink and probably needs to go home."* *OMG how am I going to get her back inside her home without her parents knowing, she exclaimed to her boyfriend!* At which point Veronica and her boyfriend assisted Johanna out the house and to Veronica's car while *Johanna was repeatedly shouting "Noooooo! Get off me!*

Somebody please help me!" Veronica thought to herself she is really out of it I wonder what she had to drink.

Veronica finally reached Johanna's house but could not find a way inside in efforts of not getting caught by her parents at 4:00 a.m. in the morning. So, they sat her down, propped her up against the front door, rang the doorbell and proceeded to Veronica's car. Johanna's mom awoke her husband and said *"someone is at the door."* He replied *"what time is it and who in the world would be coming to visit at such an odd hour in the morning."* Joseph walked down the stairs with his bat in hand, turned on the porch light and looked through the peep hole but did not see anything except an unrecognizable car leaving his driveway.

So, he started back up the stairs then he heard a small whimper coming from the base of the front door. He turned the porch light back on opened the door with bat in hand and Johanna fell backward into the house. He yelled frantically to his wife *"Hanna call the police and an ambulance its Johanna!"* Joseph's first thoughts were what's wrong with his daughter not how she got out there as he waited for the police and ambulance to come. Then he heard the rushed footsteps of his wife coming down the stairs.

When Hanna saw the state for which her daughter was in, she started to cry intensely and Joseph held her in his arms and said *"we have to believe she's going to be alright."* They did not want to take the chance of injuring her further so they kneeled on the floor and held her hand as she laid between the outside door frame and inside the house. It did not take long for the police or ambulance to get there and the EMT's got to work immediately as the police were questioning Hanna and Joseph. Joseph explained the events that led up to him finding his daughter and told them he did not have any further information.

As a result, the police left to meet back up with Johanna's parents once they arrived at the hospital in hopes of talking to Johanna once she had awakened. In the process of examining Johanna the doctor ordered toxicology blood work. The toxicology came back positive for rohypnol (commonly used as a date rape drug) and because Johanna was considered a minor, they had to get permission from her parents to conduct a sexual assault exam. Dr. Ortiz called out for the parents of Johanna, took them to a private room and shared the toxicology results then he asked for their permission to conduct a sexual assault exam. In addition, he explained if the test are conclusive, she will need other clothes to go home in because in rape cases they were required to give the victims clothing to the police after testing for evidence purposes.

In a small whimpering voice Johanna's mom asked *"can we see her after the exam,"* Dr. Ortiz said *"yes you can."* Johanna's parents stayed in the private room to console one another after hearing what has happened to their daughter then returned back to the waiting room one hour later. A few minutes later they heard their daughter screaming saying *"Noooooo! Get off me! Somebody please help me!"* Johanna's parents ran to the room where their daughter was and a nurse stopped them to say the rape exam was being conducted, so their daughter is probably having flashbacks of her assault. Being satisfied with what the nurse said they returned to their seats in the waiting room and consoled each other once more.

Dr. Ortiz came out, ushered them back into the private counseling room and explained that their daughter was indeed sexually assaulted based on the multitude of tearing and bruising possibly by more than one attacker. He also explained that Johanna was still under sedation from the drug given to her so, Johanna may not know who they were just yet. Immediately after Johanna's parents went into the room where their daughter laid but did not speak a word, they just held her hand, kissed her cheek and left to get some more clothes for her to come home in. As they were leaving the room they watched as one of the nurses placed their daughters clothes in a sealed plastic bag then in an additional brown bag before it was given to the police.

As Stacey and Peaches reached a block away from home, they went their separate ways to keep their secret. As Stacey was walking home, she had a very uneasy feeling in her stomach. But she did not let it stop her from continuing her walk home. Once she reached her house, she noticed that their trashcan was not returned to the side of the house once emptied by the city trash pickup. So, she pulled the trashcan up the driveway and returned it to its rightful place on the side of the house.

Stacey's secret meetings with Peaches was very exciting to her and it went on for three years undetected by anyone. On several occasions they would either meet at the basketball court whenever Stacey played on Saturdays or at the park where Peaches revealed her life story. With all the excitement Stacey forgot her sixteenth birthday was coming up in two days and she had not really thought about how she wanted to celebrate it. Nonetheless, she knew her father and stepmom where probably already in the planning stages.

Stacey really grew to love her stepmom Sheila because she was not over bearing and besides she made her dad very happy and that in itself was good enough for her. One day while Sheila was preparing dinner, she asked Stacey could she talk to her, Stacey replied *"yes ma'am."* Stacey had been in the kitchen with Sheila many times but this time felt different. As Sheila stirred up her gifts in the kitchen going from one place to another in the kitchen and making it all come together Sheila asked Stacey what did she want for her birthday and if it would be ok for her and her father to throw her a sweet sixteen party.

Stacey was stunned by the question of a sweet sixteen party then she told her stepmom Sheila "*I will pass on the party, but I really want a cellphone and to get my driver's license.*" Sheila was surprised when Stacey declined to have a party because what girl do anybody know that did not want a chance to dress up and get lots of gifts. Even though Sheila was shocked at Stacey's response she vaguely remembered ever seeing Stacey in a dress. Nevertheless, Sheila respected Stacey's wish and said "*okay.*"

Then Stacey remembered another reason why she connected with Sheila so well…she was not pushy and when the answer was received if and when there was a question proposed there was no push back or argument toward her answer. As a result, they were able to respect each other without thought and drew closer and closer together. Consequently, though Stacey also thought to herself what if Sheila knew she was bisexual would she still receive the same respect and love, would Sheila shy away or disconnect from Stacey all together because of her church standing.

This scared Stacey because it really felt good to have someone to talk to with no strings attached or judgement zones. After all Stacey had heard many crazy stepmom stories from her friends and she was delighted that her story differed from everyone else's. In those moments with her friends she would just lend a listening ear and console them if needed. Moreover, she did not want to add to their misery by telling them what a God-fearing down-to-earth stepmom she had.

The next day Stacey went about her day starting with school and ending with a secret after school meet up with Peaches. Once they reached their destination Stacey told Peaches her birthday was tomorrow and they would only be able to meet briefly at the basketball park. Peaches said *"are you having a party?"* Stacey replied *"no because my dad and stepmom want to throw me a sweet sixteen party can you image that?"* *"No, I cannot,"* replied Peaches and before they knew it, it was time to go.

Well, today was Stacey's birthday and all was going well with the expectation of a great evening ahead. As Stacey began getting ready for school, she danced through every step of the way with the suspense of how her birthday celebration was going to go down. She felt all tingly inside and when she opened her bedroom door there were rose pedals leading from her bedroom door down the staircase so she followed them all the way to the kitchen where the smell of breakfast was being prepared.

When she entered into the kitchen her father, both brothers and stepmom all shouted *"happy birthday!"* She saw a breakfast feast comprised of pancakes, eggs, sausages, bacon and orange juice on the table as they all sat down to eat. It was at that moment, she thought to herself how much she really loved her family and she could not imagine going through life without any of them…even her stepmom who no doubt put this all together. Stacey began thinking if they did all this for breakfast what in the world, do they have in store for her tonight. Stacey also knew the probability of her not falling asleep in class was going to be a challenge following all the good eats.

Stacey made it through all of her classes without falling asleep in anticipation of tonight's born day celebration. She wondered if she was going to receive everything she asked for and if not, what would they give her. Stacey knew for sure that her day had started with a bang and wished that her brothers would still be present at the house once she got home. That to her would be a gift in itself. As she reached the home economics class where Peaches was supposed to be, she did not see her anywhere and she began to feel sick to her stomach because she remembered the last time Peaches could not be found in class.

There was no one left in the classroom not even the teacher to ask if she came to school that morning. Stacey frantically tried to find someone from Peaches class to answer her question, but to no avail she could not find anyone. So, with her head hanging down on her way out the school doors she began thinking the worse. She pushed open the doors to exit and was startled by loud voices singing *"happy birthday to you"*…and every one of her classmates and friends from the block had a single red heart balloon even Peaches. Stacey was so overwhelmed they thought from the gesture tears started rolling down her face, but little did they know it was actually from knowing Peaches was alright.

One-by-one they individually walked up to Stacey when she reached the last step, they all had warm and fuzzy things to say to Stacey before releasing their balloon gift to her like her ability to listen without judgement, a shoulder to cry on, a true-to-life unforgettable friend, one heck of a basketball team player and genuine caring person. Stacey did not know that she meant so much to so many people and the way they all chose to show their appreciation in her mind would never be forgotten.

Stacey had so many balloons she found it difficult to see in front of her, so she had to hold her arm straight up to continue her walk home. As she and Peaches were walking home, she shared with Peaches as to why she was so overwhelmed with streaming tears rolling down her face as she walked out of the school doors. Peaches then stated in a joking manner *"so I guess it's true what they said about you…you are a genuine caring person."* Then Stacey said *"yup its official you made it into the family click and there's nothing you can do about it,"* then they continued their walk home in lots of laughter before they went their separate ways as not to get caught by Peaches stepmom.

The evening fell quickly as dinner was being placed on the beautiful decorated table by Sheila. The meal was definitely fit for kings and queens there was barbeque ribs, collard greens, candy yams, yellow rice and fried chicken. Beside each plate was crystal toasting glasses, all the dinnerware was specifically placed with candles in the middle of the table, balloons alongside the signage happy birthday and from the ceiling were all the red heart balloons Stacey received from school. Stacey's father said the blessings over the meal for the evening and Sheila tapped the side of her crystal glass to proclaim a toast.

One of her brothers walked around the table with a white towel across his arm while pouring some wine into everyone's glass as he jokingly acted like a butler saying *"sir or madam would you like some chardonnay."* As soon as everyone's glass was filled, they all went around the room making a toast to Stacey. Stacey was overwhelmed with all the love that was being displayed around the table she found herself signifying tears of joy. Thereafter, everyone started eating and telling cute stories of Stacey as she grew. Before long it was time to clean up and for Stacey's brothers to retreat to their individual homes.

Upon the next morning Stacey reminisced on her birthday celebration the night before and could not wait to share it with Peaches. It was a long day and it seemed to Stacey the day would never end. When the end of the day school bell finally rang Stacey was the first one out the door running down the hall to economics class of Peaches. Stacey was telling Peaches about last night's celebration a mile a minute as Peaches exclaims *"are you breathing?" "I am glad you had a beautiful evening though you deserve it and so much more."*

In all the excitement Stacey almost forgot to tell Peaches she also received a new cellphone and her driving lessons will begin in two weeks. At that point, Peaches reached for Stacey's hand and wrote down her telephone number in the palm of Stacey's hand. Peaches explained *"now we can have private conversations after everyone has gone*

to sleep, but I would have to call you because I do not have a cellphone so lock me in."
Then it hit Stacey so she apologized for going on and on about her event last night knowing Peaches was under such pain. Peaches explained to Stacey she was genuinely happy for Stacey even though her family life circumstances was so far from what anybody knew she was experiencing. But the flip side of it all according to Peaches she got to share it with Stacey and they will get more time together on the telephone adding a much-needed positive event in her life.

Just as they planned Peaches called Stacey that evening around 11:00 p.m. and they talked the night away until about 1:00 a.m. Within the conversation they decided to take a different route to school under the overpass of the highway and through the park. Most students did not like the route because it seemed to be the long way to school. Yet, some did use the route so they could smoke a joint before getting to school. As Stacey and Peaches were walking Stacey's phone rang.

She answered *"hello this is Stacey"* and the voice on the other end of the phone said *"did I not tell you to stay away from my daughter!*" Thereafter there were sounds of screeching tires. Stacey looked back and yelled to Peaches "it's your stepmom run!" They both started running as fast as they could, but they were no match for the car coming toward them at such an alarming rate. Peaches screamed "*I love Stacey*" then pushed Stacey as hard as she could and she took the blow from the oncoming car driven by her stepmom.

    Her stepmom kept going so Stacey was left with Peaches mangled body and as Stacey approached Peaches her eyes were open. Stacey called 911 and told the operator what happened, who did it, where they were and in an upset voice, she also told the operator "*you have got to send help now*!" She hung up the phone so she could encourage Peaches to hold on and that help was on the way. Peaches told Stacey she was sorry, but she did not want her stepmom to take anyone else from her. Stacey told her not to talk, but hold on, please hold on I can hear the ambulance coming, please hold on…Peaches made a gurgling sound then took her last breath before the ambulance could get to where they were.

The EMT tried to administer CPR on Peaches but it was too late Peaches was gone. Although Stacey was devastated, she made up in her mind that lady was not going to get away with what she had done! Along with the ambulance were the police, they got her statement and with blood saturating her shirt she rode with the police to Peaches house. When they arrived the stepmom's, car was in the driveway and she was coming out with suitcases, then Stacey pointed her out saying *"there she is!"* She then told them about Peaches disabled dad who should be in the house as well.

The police went into the house and found Peaches dad on the bed deceased…she took the time to smother him with a pillow as she tried to make her getaway and left the pillow over his face. Stacey walked over to the police car that held the stepmom and said *"lady you messed with the wrong one and I am personally going to make sure you never get out of jail, so take a real long look at this face! I am going to make sure I am at the bond hearing, trial and every future parole hearing down the road held on your behalf! You are not getting away with any of this…not on my watch, you hear me not on my watch!"*

Stacey was so angry she did not have time to process what happened until she turned the key in the door and saw Sheila. Without thinking she ran to Sheila and started crying overpoweringly. It took Sheila by surprise and then she started crying while asking Stacey where are you hurt, who did this and how did this happen? Sheila could not get an answer from Stacey so she started checking Stacey out for herself and found no injuries to her body anywhere, so she just held Stacey while she cried until she was ready to talk.

It looked like Stacey was going into shock so she called 911 emergency, her husband and Stacey's brothers. All Sheila could think about was bringing God into the situation while she waited for an ambulance to get there. Once the ambulance arrived, they too did not find any wounds or injuries just Stacey's shirt saturated with blood. So, the police was called because of the strange circumstances.

The rest of the family showed up one by one, but the only person who could give them answers was lying in a hospital bed with her eyes open uttering not a word just a frozen stare. The police arrived and realized after they saw Stacey that she was the same young lady who helped them catch a double homicide murderer that morning. At that point, the police informed Stacey's family how brave she was this morning and how her schoolmate was one of the murdered victims.

    After the shooting was over a woman ran out of her home and shouted "someone call 911 two children have been shot"! When she made her statement more people began coming out of their homes to try and see if they could be of help to Macaela and her brother. One of the neighborhood residents recognized whose children they were and ran to inform their parents. But when he got there no one was home so he ran back to the scene so he could give the information to the police once they arrived.

    When he returned to the scene people from all walks of life were either praying aloud or crying and saying *"this should not be, this just should not be this is our neighborhood."* Once the police arrived, they saw the children laying on the sidewalk bleeding plentifully in their own blood , unconscious and holding hands. It did not take long for some of the officers to get choked up about what they were seeing, but it did not stop them from clearing the way for the EMT's. Once the way was cleared for the EMT's they too could not help but look at each other for a short minute with tears in their eyes. Then an officer shouted "*does anyone have any idea who these children are*" and the gentleman who ran to the house of Macaela and Abdu stated "*I do.*"

    Then the gentleman later identified as Mr. Peters who was the janitor where the children lived told the officers what they needed to know. Mr. Peters explained that he ran to the children's home but there was no answer so, he returned to the scene. Nevertheless, Mr. Peters accompanied the police in leading them to Macaela and Abdu's home after one of the officers asked the EMT which hospital where they taking the children to.

    Mr. Peters and Officer O'Connor sat for a short while in front of Macaela and Abdu's home then Mr. Peters noticed the mom's vehicle pulling up in front of the apartment building. As Mr. Peters and Officer O'Connor were making their way to the car the children's mom Adaego was stepping out of her car. When they approached Macaela's mom Adaego Officer O'Connor introduced himself then explained why he was there and immediately Adaego called her husband Idunnuola to inform him of what has happen in addition to having him meet her at the hospital.

     Once Adaego finished the conversation with her husband Officer O'Connor asked Adaego can he escort her to the hospital where her children were so, she could get to the hospital faster, Adaego replied *"yes please"* in a trembling voice. Adaego knew how to trust the direction of God by praying before she got to the hospital. She also prayed that this would not be a teaching moment and lose both of her children in the process. By the time she and Officer O'Connor reached the hospital Adaego noticed her husband's work truck.

     When the parents saw one another, they embraced and headed toward the emergency room nurses station to inquire which room their children were being kept. At which time they were told the children were in two separate rooms, but right next door to one another. Adaego and Idunnuola entered into Abdu's room first. They were shocked by all the wires attached to their son and the bandages on his left leg. As Idunnuola made his way around the hospital bed he kissed his son's forehead then reached for his hand and expressed to his wife *"we need to pray"*.

Once they finished praying for Abdu, they kissed his forehead and left the room to go check on Macaela. When they got to Macaela's room she also was connected to many machines with wires and a bandage going around her head. Adaego began to think it was just this morning she and her daughter were laughing and now she is looking at her daughter laying very still in a hospital bed. Once again Idunnuola expressed to his wife Adaego that they needed to pray. So, they prayed for Macaela and asked that God's will be done.

They opened their eyes and saw a doctor standing in the doorway who also stated *"amen"* once the prayer was completed. However, they did not acknowledge the doctor until they kissed Macaela's forehead then held her hand to let her know she was not alone. It was at this point they acknowledged Dr. Ephraim and without delay they wanted answers on their children's status. Dr. Ephraim explained that Macaela was in a drug induced coma to prevent any further swelling because she has a bullet lodged in her head in an awkward position that makes it very dangerous to operate right now. He further explained it is a waiting game at the moment to see if the bullet will move on its own allowing them to remove the bullet quickly and safely.

However, I regret to inform you that Abdu lost a lot of blood prior to getting here, he may lose his leg or succumb to his injuries because he had two bullets that pierced a main artery in his leg. This gives him a 20/40 chance of survival rate and it is nothing short of a miracle that he is still with us. Dr. Ephraim additionally explained that him and his medical staff members are hopeful both children are going to pull through and they were going to do everything possible to make sure of it, then departed from the parents.

It had been two months after the shooting and Macaela was still in a coma even after the bullet was removed the month prior to the current visit of her parents that day. In waiting for her to return back to them her parents took turns every evening sitting by her bed praying, singing and holding her hand to ensure she could feel someone was with her. Little did they know today would be the day Macaela stirred from her coma all because she heard her brothers voice talking and talking as usual. Subsequently, though and at that point she was elated to hear her brothers voice because that meant they had survived their ordeal. She opened her mouth to say *"Abdu can a girl get some sleep around here please stop talking"* and then she opened her eyes.

Her mother jumped up and started calling for the nurse and when the nurse got to the room, she checked Macaela's vital signs then called Dr. Ephraim to report Macaela has awaken. Dr Ephraim stated *"I am on my way."* Macaela called her husband Idunnuola and he to stated he was on his way. Macaela's father got there very quickly and for the first time Macaela watched as her parents embrace one another while crying. Then they began to tell

Macaela how long she was in a coma and because the bullet that was lodged in her head moved on its own a surgery was performed to save her life.

Then Macaela asked her mom "where is Abdu I heard him loudly talking to you from the moon and back." Her parents looked at each other and then Macaela with such concern. Her mom responded in a trembling voice *"Abdu was called home a month ago because of a blood clot that traveled to his lung from bullets that entered his main artery."* Macaela screamed so loud several nurses came running into her hospital room. They had to sedate Macaela because she started shouting *"it's my fault I'm sorry mommy and daddy then she snatched out her IV"* all the while crying hysterically and before anyone knew it the medication had taken its course which caused Macaela to drift off to sleep.

Macaela parents called out to Jesus in prayer to *"save their daughter during their time of affliction, let not this affliction have charge over her, deliver her from the evil that has taken place in their lives and bring her back to us in her right mind because we know you will turn this evil into good for your glory. Amen."*

Macaela's parents had a relationship with God and remembered his promise as he spoke to Joshua that as he was with Moses, so will I be with you; I will never leave you or forsake you (Joshua 1:5 NIV). They always knew that God was their present-day help and there was nothing the doctors could do, so they sought out the greatest physician of them all! They also knew that God was no respecter of persons, so they made a choice to trust God instead of the situation.

The Meeting

Unique successfully completed her plan of returning her grades to where they needed to be in efforts of being promoted. She marveled at her skill-set to get the job done, her ability to stay focus and the fact that she did it on her own in spite of her circumstances. Unique felt if she stayed focused on the prize (graduating from high school) she can then move out on her own. Unique started feeling abandoned by her mom and sister because she had yet to hear from either of them or even how Porsha was doing. She tried not to let it bother her but it did because she wanted to share her good news with somebody…or anybody that in the least cared.

A whole year had passed and it was now time for Unique to graduate from high school. After summer school Unique surrounded herself with people who encouraged her to keep pressing toward her intended goal of graduating from high school. Although there was still no word on the whereabouts of her mom or sister, she had befriended Melody a classmate from school, they got really close, so Melody's mom took them shopping to get all the necessities for graduation day. Unique was still babysitting so all of her necessities were covered.

Unique wanted someone to represent her as a family member at the graduation, so she had planned to tell her dad once she returned home. However, when she got home his car was gone, there was a note on the refrigerator stating he went on a trip with Lyla (his lady friend) and would return a week or so. Unique once again received a note of abandonment and she just could not believe it was happening again before her very important day. The feeling of insignificance fell hard on her heart for a second time rearing its ugly head. Only this time instead of trying to end her life she called her friend Melody who always had the right words to calm her raging thoughts.

Unique and Melody talked and cried a long while. When Melody felt everything was good enough for them to now go to sleep, they said their goodnights and hung up the phone. On the other hand, Unique could not sleep just then so she just laid on her bed in her thoughts. Slowly Unique eyes got heavy and she began to dream. The dream consisted of her getting ready for her important day, but she started to cry yelling *"what's the point of doing all of this when no one cared enough to celebrate her*!" She took off running toward the window in her graduation attire and then she woke up abruptly after she heard a voice say "***I will never leave you nor forsake you***" (Deuteronomy 31:6 NIV).

Unique curled herself up and rocked herself back to sleep being very afraid. Then an hour or two later her alarm clock went off. She got up in disbelief thinking it was all a dream, so she walked down the hall to her father's bedroom to ask him will he be attending her graduation, she knocked repeatedly and because of no answer she opened the door while calling out to him. When the door was finally opened the bed had not been slept in, all of his clothes were gone and nothing was left in the dresser drawers. Then she yelled aloud in anger "*I hate you and I am not going to let you ruin my day…I am not!*"

Unique took off running down the hall into her bedroom got herself together, put her graduation attire on and called Melody to get a ride. Unique's anguish had now turned to anger. Unique had arrived at the school, thanked Melody's mom and dad then she told Melody she would meet her in the classroom as she was making her way to the restroom. She cried silently so no one would hear her because she just did not understand why these things were happening to her and why now.

As the ceremony took place Unique was fighting back tears when her name was called as she reached for her high school diploma. She was very angry but decided to put on a fake smile to get her through the commemorative event. As she was making her way back to her seat, she saw a silhouette at the back door holding the hand of a small child. At last the ceremony was over so she frantically made her way to the back door thus making out the silhouettes to be her sister and Porsha. But where was mom…she thought.

Upon trying to reach them, Porsha was already making her way to Unique, jumped in Unique's arms and gave her the biggest longest hug accompanied with lots of kisses. At that moment the tears started to flow down Unique's face then she told her sister lets go somewhere quiet after asking her *"where is mom?"* When they walked out the building, she saw her mother's car then asked her sister again "where is mom?" Then her sister said *"mom is in a domestic violence program in efforts of dad not finding her and I was so scared after what I witnessed, I ran back to my former boyfriends apartment where I have been living since the incident. Then she said mom signed over her car to me so I could have transportation for Porsha and I."*

Then Unique said *"what about me? You came to my school today and you did not think to reach out to me to let me know what was going on? Did anyone think about what dad would do to me not being able to find mom?*

It's been well over a year and I have received not a word from anybody, so I began to think the worse. Did anyone think about me"? Do you know I tried to take myself out of this world twice because I did not think anyone cared, wanted me or loved me enough to come see about me and to know

now you were not far away just downtown from the house!"

"How am I supposed to process all of this on a day I should be celebrating my graduation. Do you even care that daddy has now abandoned me and I do not see any signs of him coming back based on a letter he too left for me to find! Tell me who thought about me and my wellbeing…tell me who?"

Then her sister said "I am truly sorry, but I was scared". Then Unique said "soooo you not scared today? Look sis this is my cellphone number so we can perhaps keep in touch just so you know I am alright after today, thanks for coming" and then she reached for Porsha gave her a huge hug with lots of kisses at that juncture then she walked away. Unique did not want to spoil Melody's graduation moment so she walked all the way home in her anger.

When Unique finally reached home there was an eviction notice on the door and each day after that all the utilities were being cut off one-by-one with a deadline for the lights 5:00 p.m. that day. These events fueled Unique's anger and she knew she had to reach out to someone fast. Well she called the only friend that knew her and immediately Melody asked Unique if it was okay to tell her mom and dad, Unique said *"yes."*

Melody and her family came over and helped her get the bulk of her belongings then Melody's mom walked over to Unique and said "I am so sorry this has happened…*you are staying with us and please know you will not be in the way."* When they reached Melody's family home her mom walked her upstairs to a bedroom next to Melody. She stated it was her older son's childhood room who now lives in Canada as a teacher. Unique gave her a hug and said "thank you," then Melody helped her put her belongings away. Before long it was time to go to bed.

At the breakfast table Melody exclaimed she was so happy to have her best friend living with her. Immediately after Melody's mom Tasha asked Unique *"are you going to be okay with going to church with us on Sundays"* and Unique replied "no ma'am that would not be a problem at all." Then Unique thanked everyone for allowing her to stay in their home. Everyone chimed *"you are most welcome anytime."* Both Melody and Unique had secured summer jobs midway through their graduating month so immediately after breakfast Tasha dropped them off at the mall to start their first day.

After such a grueling week Unique still needed to purchase a couple of outfits for church on Sundays, so Melody accompanied her. Melody also explained that she did not have to get all gussied up because their pastor believed that we should come as we are, but decent and in order. Unique asked Melody not to laugh at her but "*what does decent and in order mean.*" Melody answered and said "it means no revealing clothing". "*Oh, so the girls have to be in hiding, skirts must be length appropriate not showcasing our she shed and no air-conditioned jeans,*" Unique said jokingly. Melody said "*you got it in a nut shell*" and they both laughed their way to the next store. Unique was able to find some very comfortable apparel to meet the standards of church attire and they began their way home.

Unique had never been to church before and did not know what to expect. When they got their that Sunday morning everyone was very cordial. Everyone was ushered to their seat except Melody. She did not see which way Melody went but she was sure she would be back. Then Unique noticed when they got to their seating everyone had to move all the way down the row of seats to allow other members or visitors room enough to sit.

Beforehand it was time for church to begin. The church setting was somewhat similar to Unique's graduation ceremony and she began to drift off to that day and how furiously discouraged she was with the answers to the questions she asked her sister. At that moment the choir started singing and it was the lead singer that got her attention…it was Melody. Unique never heard anything so beautiful in the way that it touched her heart not because she knew who the singer was but because it began to feel like everything was going to be okay. Immediately after Pastor Ralph got up and started preaching with a message entitled "You Are Not Alone".

Pastor Ralph talked about this man named Jesus and how he would be with us always never forsaking us and the part that got the hairs on Unique's neck to stand up was this Jesus wanted them to "come unto him, all ye that labour and are heavy laden, and he would give us rest" (Matthew 11:28 KJV). She remembered those words within the two times she tried to commit suicide and she knew Melody did not tell anyone because she never shared that part of her life with anyone, not even Melody. Once the sermon was over, Pastor Ralph conducted an alter call for anyone that wanted to give their life to Christ Jesus. Many people took the walk down to the alter apart from Unique because she simply did not know what that meant.

When church was over and on Unique's way out the door, she saw her friend Melody. *She said "girl you did not tell me you could sing I mean sang OMG, it was beautiful!"* Melody replied *"thank you and it took a numerous amount of years for me to get out of my comfort zone to sing in front of other people. Although I appreciate your admirations, however I cannot take the credit it was Jesus who showed me the way and I believe that Jesus will someday show you the way as well."* Unique did not reply.

After delivering the prognosis of Cosandra he excused himself then Mary immediately in full swing began crying excessively. Against her fleshly judgement Antionette went over to Mary to say "*I am deeply sorry because had I not brought Cosandra with me she would not be fighting for her life right now."* Then Mary answered *"all of this is my fault and I am terrified that I am going to have to pay for what I have done through Cosandra. I do not want to lose her."* Antionette responded by saying *"I cannot even phantom the thought, so you are going to give as much blood as humanly possible for the sake of Cosandra…okay?"*

      As both Mary and Antionette made their way to the blood work laboratory there was no further conversation. Once inside the laboratory they discovered everyone had to wait their individual turns for there was a multitude of other people abroad getting blood work done. Finally, and after twenty-five minutes of waiting it was Mary's turn to give blood. She asked how long would it take because she had to get back upstairs to her daughter and the technician explained it would take approximately 10 to 15 minutes. Too much of Mary's surprise and without any delay it was over. At which point Mary was given some crackers and juice to replenish the loss of fluid and away they went returning to the emergency ICU room where Cosandra was being kept until further notice.

Unfortunately, there was still no communication between Mary and Antionette perhaps because of either the equaled guilt they felt individually or the unforgiveness seed currently in their hearts as to how the issue at hand came about. How were they going to be a force to be reckoned with through prayer for the sake of Cosandra without forgiveness toward one another? Well I can tell you...they will not be able to.

In order for love to annihilate the seed of unforgiveness somebody has to initiate it without feeling like it is all about them. In other words, someone has got to be the better person and realize that unless unforgiveness is removed from the equation God will not move. Why, because there is no true humbleness in the balance it is just...what about me syndrome.

Not forgetting the fact that if we do not forgive God cannot forgive us in "all" of our wrong doings through life (Matthew 6:14-15 NIV). However, if you want to remain in the wilderness without passing the test of God's instruction, passion and order then have at it. Do you not know that you will remain in the wilderness knowing that all of your prayers and blessing will be delayed or not answered?

Was Mary or Antionette ever made aware of this? Did they not think for a moment that Cosandra's life could be hanging in the balance based on their inability to forgive? So, tell me are you going to let unforgiveness stop you from prospering? No, I would think not. Me, personally haven already been through this multiple times…I will take forgiveness at any given moment for two hundred as they say in the game of jeopardy.

Conversely though, it was touch and go for Cosandra all evening into the morning dew when Mary was awakened by the doctor to remark that Mary was not a match for Cosandra's rare O negative blood type so they could not use her blood being B positive. Baffled but understandingly so Mary told the doctor she was so sorry and had forgotten through all the commotion that Cosandra was adopted as a baby because she has Mayer-Rokitansky-Küster-Hauser (MRKH) syndrome. In simpler terms it means she was born with no uterus. As Antionette listened with astonishment her concern for Cosandra's survival intensified. Antionette knew O blood type whether negative or positive was a scarcity.

The doctor responded, "*I regret to inform you Cosandra's chances of survival would not be great when we have to operate if we do not have sufficient blood on hand*". Out of terror and anxiety Antionette said "*I do not know what my blood type is but I would like to be tested*"! Then and there is when Mary and Antionette's eyes locked as a way of Antionette saying please let me do this.

Mary nodded yes in agreement and just like Antionette escorted Mary down to the blood work laboratory Mary did the same for Antionette. Only this time when the procedure was over and they were in the elevator to return to the emergency ICU floor Mary said "*even if after all of this and your blood type is not what I need I want to say thank you. In addition, you have no reason to forgive me, but will you ever forgive me.*"

Antionette looked at Mary for a brief moment and said "yes, and will you be able to forgive me for my part in this." At that moment Mary embraced Antionette and said "*of course, I do not know what I would have done if you were not here."* They both cried within their embrace and as they were making their way down the hall, they noticed Cosandra was being moved out of her room speedily. They ran the rest of the way and was approached by the assigned nurse to Cosandra who began explaining that Cosandra was on her way to emergency surgery. Adding it would also be a couple of hours before they would know the outcome.

    Confronted by the possibility of losing Cosandra Mary asked if there was a chapel within the hospital although she had not practiced her faith in a very long time. The nurse directed them to the first floor, gave them both a card entitled "Real Women Real Talk Outreach Ministry" with a scripture on the back saying Matthew 11:28 then pointed them in the right direction. Once Mary and Antoinette reached the chapel, they both knelt down at the altar, completed their own individual prayers unto God on behalf of Cosandra then individually asked God for forgiveness.

    When Johanna's parents finally reached their home, they were reminded again of the scene that involved their daughter once they crossed over the threshold of the entrance doorway. Johanna's father told his wife he would wait downstairs while she went upstairs to get Johanna some clothes. As Joseph sat waiting on his wife Hanna multiple questions entered his thought pattern aloud like; who placed Johanna at the door? When did she leave the house? Where did she go?

Who would do such a thing to his daughter? Then he asked God why did he let this happen to his dear sweet Johanna? He also questioned himself if he would be able to trust Johanna again. He also began to blame himself for not protecting his daughter as a parent should. There were no immediate answers so he began to weep for the pain his daughter endured.

Joseph blamed himself for not knowing his daughter better instead of assuming because she was a good girl academically that a one-on-one conversation with his daughter was not necessary. Hanna was standing on the staircase listening to her husband and when she thought it was okay to enter the family room as not to interrupt Joseph's time with his thoughts or God, only then did she continue down the staircase. Straightaway after noticing his wife Hanna entering the family room they left to return to the hospital.

Once Joseph parked the car he got out, opened the door for his wife, and then he reached for her hand so they could walk in unity. Joseph was a wise man and he knew the way to get through this was with his wife Hanna at his side. He knew he could count on his wife, help mate and the love of his life. Above all he knew the key to being triumph in any situation as man and wife is to make sure they stood on the fact each should always be a part of the decision-making process.

Johanna had been through the worst with the drug given to her at the party and was finally coming out of it, but there was still some apparent grogginess. The nurse assigned to Johanna asked Joseph and Hanna was Johanna on birth control pills. Hanna answered and said *"yes we started her on birth control when she turned thirteen years of age."* I commend you both on your decision stated the nurse, but may I ask why at thirteen." Then Joseph answered *"when talks began in our governmental offices to give teenagers the right to withhold sexual and drug use from their parents we knew we had to protect our child with an explanation as to why no good thing would come from it and she could be bound to a decision emotionally she was not ready for."*

At that moment, Johanna woke up saying hi mom and dad *"where am I"* in a groggy voice? *You are in the hospital and we will explain later, replied Hanna.* Eventually Johanna was released that evening to go home. Once there it was decided that Hanna would take an emergency leave of absence and Joseph would continue to work because of his significant income base. They were given a calming medication prescription just in case Johanna started having episodes of what happened to her.

As Joseph was driving home Johanna fell asleep during the ride and awakened in time to go inside the house. Johanna exclaimed *"I do not know why I am so sleepy but do you guys mind if I go to bed after we eat?"* Johanna's mom said *"not a problem baby I will make your favorite cubed chicken, yellow rice and spinach medley."* After dinner was cooked and they sat at the table as a family Johanna said goodnight once done while Joseph collected the dishes so he could wash them before him and Hanna turned in for the evening themselves. They did not realize how tired they were so sleep came quickly for the both of them.

However, within two hours of going to bed both Hanna and Joseph heard screams coming from Johanna's room so both parents ran down to their daughter's room to see what was going on. When they opened the door, Johanna was fighting in her sleep and saying *"Noooooo! Get off me! Somebody help me please*!" Joseph awakened Johanna and immediately after Johanna asked her parents *"what was wrong and why were they in her room."*

At that point, Hanna decided that it was time to let Johanna know what had happened to her and how she was discovered. Joseph left the room so mother and daughter could have some space during their conversation. As Hanna was informing Johanna tears began to fall down Johanna's cheeks. Immediately after Hanna just held Johanna in her arms as she wept.   Johanna cried herself to sleep and when the coast was clear Hanna returned to her bedroom and found that Joseph was waiting up so he could console his wife.

The next day Hanna arose to fix breakfast and she walked down to Johanna's bedroom to see what she had a taste for that morning. When Hanna knocked on the door several times there was no answer so she decided to walk in. As soon as she entered calling out to Johanna, she saw Johanna sitting up in the bed holding her legs close to her chest rocking back and forth. As Hanna called out to Johanna in a soft voice at first there was no response, but when she moved closer Johanna spoke. She said *"mom I am scared to go to sleep because since you told me what happened to me, I am starting to see image pieces that just do not make since."*

Hanna then explained to her daughter in hopes of bringing all those pieces together to get some justice for you realizing it is not going to happen as fast as we would like. I would like to have you talk to someone outside of me or your dad in efforts of getting the help you need to get you through this. We prayed that God would lead us as to who would be best to send you to. You see while at the hospital I removed a card from behind the bathroom stall door entitled "Real Women Real Talk Outreach Ministry", but what got my attention was the reverse side of the card that said "**come unto me, all ye that labour and are heavy laden, and I will give you rest…Matthew 11:28.**" I have met with the founder so; with your permission I would like to sign you up for a one-on-one session with her; Johanna replied I do not know mom but if you think it will help, okay.

While they were eating Johanna asked her mom "*has Veronica been by the house?*" Hanna replied "*no baby she has not been here in a while as best I can remember.*" Johanna remembered that she and Veronica were inseparable besties. Johanna decided after breakfast she would give Veronica a call but did not remember seeing her personal phone when she returned home. Then she asked her mom did she know the location of her cellphone and her mom answered no baby I have not seen it.

After they were finished eating Johanna offered to wash the dishes to keep her mind off her torment. It was then Hanna told Johanna she took a leave of absence so she could help her through this wicked situation.

Then Johanna started to cry and then her mom said I did not mean to make you cry...I am so sorry. Johanna said "*mom it's not you I am upset because I just cannot remember and based on what you told me as to what happened to me, I do not know if I ever want to know or go through it again.*"

"*I cannot remember where I was, who I was with or who hated me so much that they would assault me!*" Hanna then told Johanna I would not want to go through it either and that is why I am here so you do not have to go through it alone. Your father and I cannot put our heads around any of this but we will do whatever it takes to get you through this. Johanna then told her mom that she was going to go upstairs and look for her cellphone so she could call Veronica.

Johanna tore her room up but could not find her phone. When she deemed, she was finished looking she thought she would just speak with Veronica on Sunday when she goes to church with her parents. Johanna was in her room for so long looking for her cellphone it was almost dinner time. Johanna went back downstairs where her mom was cooking dinner. Then Johanna asked her mom "what if this was all my fault would you still love me?" Then Hanna turned and faced her daughter and said *"baby there is nothing in this world that would make me stop loving you…we all have fallen short of God's glory in some form or fashion. Johanna maybe you made a choice which did not work in your favor but this is not your fault nor did you deserve what happened to you and we are going to be with you every step of the way no matter where the truth may lead."*

    Johanna felt the need to give her mother a hug as she was mentally thanking God for the parents, he had blessed her with. She knew this could have turned out a different way that would have pushed her into hating to come home, herself, and her parents. Johanna felt loved, supported and she knew that she would have to earn her parents trust going forward. Johanna knew this was not going to be an easy task especially with her father.

    Deep down inside Johanna knew her parents were really hurting from the situation at hand and because there were no clear answers it broke her heart that she had hurt her parents. This was one of the hardest things to come to grips with and Johanna did not know if she could ever forgive herself for what she put her parents through. Before the negative thoughts could take over her father walked in from work and stated *"how are my favorite two ladies in the whole wide world doing this evening?"* Johanna's mom said *"great now that you are home!"* However, Johanna looked at her dad with tears in her eyes and said "I am so sorry daddy" then ran upstairs crying aloud as she made her way to her room.

    Joseph went upstairs after Johanna and explained to her that he was not angry at her because of what happened, but he was upset with himself because he felt he could have protected her better. Although her father tried his hardest to get Johanna to forgive herself and come back downstairs to eat dinner it did not happen. So, Joseph excused himself, took a shower then proceeded downstairs to eat dinner in hopes of seeing Johanna already at the table. Hanna and Joseph ate dinner without Johanna that evening.

    When Hanna checked on Johanna before going to bed, she saw that Johanna was sleeping so she closed the door and walked back down the hall to her own bedroom. Little did she know Johanna was awake pretending to be sleep because she was still too scared to go to sleep. Johanna stayed up all night and decided to get her clothes ready for church once she started seeing the peeks of daylight. Immediately after she went downstairs, fixed her some cereal for breakfast and remained downstairs waiting for her parents to join her.

Her dad said "*good morning baby girl*" and her mom said "*don't you look pretty.*" Johanna replied "*good morning. I apologize for leaving and not having dinner with you.*" Joseph then said "*we understand and we love you.*" They gave Johanna a group hug and off they went to church. Johanna was determined to find some answers to her situation and she just knew Veronica could help her figure it out so she became very apprehensive in getting to church.

Johanna had not bumped into Veronica while entering the church so she planned to look for her after service. Johanna could not comprehend the message or what the speaker was trying to portray since her thoughts were on finding Veronica after church and what she would say once she found her. At last the sermon was over, she explained to her mom she was going to find Veronica and she would meet them at the car in about fifteen minutes. Hanna said "no problem baby."

As a final point Johanna could not find Veronica until she started out to the parking lot. She took off running to catch up to her and once she got close enough to Veronica, she called out to her. Veronica recognized the voice and turned to see that it was her bestie Johanna. They hugged and Veronica said "*girl where have you been, I have been calling you.*" Johanna said "*I need to talk to you.*"

Veronica said *anything for my girl, I am free now* what's up. Johanna said "*let me tell my parents we are going to have lunch and you will bring me home is that okay.*" Veronica, exclaimed excitedly "*what is wrong with you of course it is okay!*" Once they reached their favorite mom and pop restaurant Johanna asked "*did we do anything or go anywhere last weekend and if so, can you tell me where we went and if anything happened.*"

As Veronica told the events of the evening from beginning to end.

Tears began to form in Johanna's eyes. Veronica stopped talking and asked Johanna what was wrong. Johanna said "*so it was you who left me on the threshold of my house for my parents to find?*" Veronica then stated "*I tried to find a way into your room but it was too high to carry you up without a latter then I checked other locations but could not find any so, I rang the front door bell for one of your parents to let you in*". Johanna explained to Veronica that she ended up in the hospital because she was sexually assaulted that night and she is still trying to put all the pieces together but was having a hard time due to a date rape drug she was given.

Veronica started crying telling Johanna how sorry she was and had she known she would have called the police herself! She also said "*when I saw Mike and Evan bringing you downstairs Mike said you had too much to drink and I should probably take you home…OMG Johanna I am so sorry!*" Then Johanna stood up from the table and asked Veronica to please take her home. Veronica did not know what else to say to Johanna especially when it was her who convinced Johanna to go to Mike's party to watch her back. Words could not describe how bad Veronica was feeling because she knew her friend was feeling worse. When Veronica reached Johanna's house and before Johanna stepped out of her car, she told Johanna *"once you piece all this together please let me know so I can testify."*

Johanna felt numb and could not find the energy to answer so she just closed the car door then proceeded to the front door of her house. Johanna passed out into her father's arms as he watched a familiar car make its way out of their driveway. Joseph managed to pick his daughter up, place her on the family room couch, called to his wife and then Hanna called for an ambulance.

Once they got to the hospital and Johanna was seen by the doctor Johanna was diagnosed with exhaustion. It was then Johanna's parents explained what happened to Johanna and how she told her mom she was afraid to go to sleep. Johanna was prescribed some sleeping pills to help her rest and immediately after she was discharged. Johanna woke up during the ride home staring blankly out the window and did not say a word. Upon reaching home Johanna got out, went into the house and retired to her bedroom.

A few minutes later Hanna came upstairs to Johanna's room to give her the medicine prescribed with a glass of water. When Hanna reached the bedroom, she shared with Joseph he asked if she knew the person who brought Johanna home after church. Hanna said *"yes, it was her best friend Veronica."* It was then he told Hanna that was the same car he saw driving out of their driveway when he found Johanna at the front door. Then Hanna said *"I do not know how but somehow I will make an attempt to speak with Veronica alone so we can finally get some answers.*

Stacey's family sat next to her hospital bed trying to comprehend and process what their loved one had undergone. Everyone watched Stacey with great concern praying she was going to return to them being the Stacey that they all knew and loved. Dr. Brown came into Stacey's room to report that Stacey was indeed in psychological shock due to the stressful event of watching her classmate die in her arms. As a precaution we are going to keep Stacy overnight for observation to allow the stress hormones that have been released into her bloodstream to decrease. Dr. Brown also mentioned that he could only authorize the parents for overnight stay with the patient.

It was decided that Stacey's father Brooklyn and stepmom Sheila would be the ones to stay over. Both of Stacey's brothers Christopher and David left feeling very proud of their little sister in her part of helping the police catch a double homicide murderer. At the same time, they were also concerned about her mental stability moving forward having lost her best friend in the nightmare with no certainty how she will be able to cope with it.

Nonetheless, they both vowed they would be there for her to help her cope with loss because they knew firsthand what it took after losing their biological mom. Meanwhile back at the hospital Brooklyn and Sheila were reminiscing on the birthday evening they spent family time with Stacey. Brooklyn additionally began thinking about the time she was born and asked himself how was he going to raise his two sons and now a newborn baby girl without their mom. Then he gave himself an imaginary pat on the back because he managed to raise her for sixteen years and she turned out to be a very remarkable young lady.

Sheila excused herself to go to the ladies room and one of the nurses saw that she was crying then followed Sheila to offer her some encouraging prayer during her time of need. Nurse Barbara thanked Sheila for allowing her to pray over the situation with Stacey after the prayer was completed. She also stated *"considering how close Stacey was with one of the victims she might need to talk through it in a group setting or in a one-on-one session"*. Then she gave Sheila a card entitled "Real Women Real Talk Outreach Ministry" and explained that she met the founder at a shelter while she was voluntarily ministering the Word of God.

Nurse Barbara went on to say her niece went through something traumatic and because her niece was not eighteen yet she had a one-on-one session with the founder instead of a group session. Nonetheless, there was a noticeable change in her niece for the better and she would love to see the same outcome for Stacey. Sheila knew in her heart nurse Barbara was an answer to her prayers and accepted the card as a confirmation that Stacey was going to be alright.

Macaela woke up feeling very drained, tied to her hospital bed and she started crying in disbelief that she was not going to see or hear her brother talking with no end again. Adaego awakened from the reclining chair she fell asleep in when she heard Macaela crying . As she embraced her daughter Macaela said *"mom I am especially hurt for the mere reason I did not get to say goodbye, I feel responsible for the death of my brother because of the many times I used to wish he would simply be quiet and now I wish I could take it all back just to have him back in our lives again. Yet it was his ongoing chatter I heard which helped me find my way out of the coma."*

Mom what am I supposed to do now? I cannot go on in life like he did not exist? Why did God let this happen? Oh, mama why? Adaego replied *"Baby, I cannot begin to know what it must be for you as you went through this traumatic experience, but I am confident that as we as a family go through the healing process the answers will be revealed".*

Nothing pains me more than to know your brother is no longer with us in body, but I am grateful that it was your brothers spirit that brought you back to us. Perhaps God did not want him to suffer through life because of his injuries and chose to bring him home so he can be made whole again. Please know that I and your father share the same grief with you thus also knowing the healing process is going to take time. As a result, I have joined a women's group that I believe will help me to continue to be strong in the Lord and in the power of his might. When you are ready Real Women Real Talk Outreach Ministry has a place for you as well."

After a couple of weeks Macaela was released from the hospital and when she got home, she saw a neighborhood make shift memorial made up of flowers, teddy bears, candles and a tennis racket along the fence of their apartment building in honor of her brother. She also noticed her parents had enlarged and donated Abdu's last school picture. Adaego told Macaela people were coming from miles around each day just to show their condolences. There were many people coming every day that came who did not live in the nearby neighborhoods but heard the story of my babies holding hands as they laid fighting for life. At first your father and I were very upset to hear the story on how our children were displayed on the sidewalk while the perpetrators ran away like cowards but through much prayer, we are learning each day to focus on the love that was being interpreted to the world by the holding of your hands.

As they made their way upstairs Adaego then said Macaela *"this is by no means easy to endure baby your father and I cry every day for the void we feel in our hearts and although we know God has a purpose for all of this…we are still human struggling to understand"*. "So, I encourage you not to wait too long before talking to someone to start your healing process to maintain your peace of mind. This is something we cannot go through alone and I know it is harder for you because you were there. I want us to get through this together, okay."   Yes, ma'am I understand, whispered Macaela.

The Exit

Unique and Melody spent a lot of time together which gave Unique a since of sisterhood between them, but that did not take the place of her biological family. She longed to have what Melody had because they made her feel like she belonged. Unique knew being with them and going to church helped her not to be so angry at her situation. Unique often thought to herself what was going to happen to her once she moved out on her own and who would help her get rid of the inferno of anger within her.

Unique's thoughts were interrupted by a knock on her bedroom door, it was Melody. She asked Melody to come in and once they got their chatter going Melody asked Unique if she would like to join her and some of the church choir members in volunteering at a homeless shelter for women. Unique answered *"sure and what will we be doing because a sister cannot sing."*

Melody laughed then said "I would never put you on the spot like that. While some choir members will be singing the rest of us will be cooking a pre-planned breakfast." Unique said *"now that I can do…what time should I be ready."* Melody came back with *"I know tomorrow is our first Saturday off but we must prepare ourselves for an 8:30am pick up to serve the women and children by 10:00am."*

The evening had come and gone. It was now time to get up for the church homeless shelter event. She and Melody were picked up promptly. The choir sang all the way there which put great joy in the heart of Unique to somewhat be a part of something so encouraging. Unique felt like she could listen to them all day and never get tired of such beauty.

After breakfast was finished being prepared it was now time to serve and the three choir members ended their last song, then began to serve the familics. As they were serving a distinguished woman came in and introduced herself as the founder of "Real Women Real Talk Outreach Ministry" and that she was there to deliver a message entitled "What Is Your Dis-ease" coming from Mark

11:25 KJV. She went on to explain that a disease as we know is a disorder of structure or function in a human.

She continued and said *"unfortunately, there are people or situations in our lives that have either disappointed us, used us, abused us, lied to us and abandoned us. However, I am here today to ask you how long are you going to let people or situations to steal the joy that is rightfully yours. You see every day that you hold unto a negative situation or what someone has done or said to you, you are allowing them to steal your joy"*.

To that I say let go and let God! We were not designed to hold grudges or to live life in anger. We were designed to love as God loves. God so loved the world he gave his only begotten son (John 3:16 KJV) who did no wrong. If we get up every day in his grace and mercy not forgiving others, we are leaving the door wide open for God not to forgive us.

So, I ask you what is your dis-ease. Is it pride, stubbornness, lack of belief or are you okay with the anger that is consuming your life and heart? Right now, you are in your personal wilderness and it is time to look for the exit door!

Who is worth losing all that God has for you? Where you are today does not mean you are bound there, He has something better for you, but you have to let go of what got you there and has caused you to be so angry. The world did not give us our joy and we should not allow it or them to take it away! If I am talking to you say this prayer with me:

"Father in heaven, I am a sinner seeking your face because of my unforgiving heart. I want to know you better so I willingly give my thoughts, behavior, words and heart to you to use as you consider necessary. Father, please remove and free me from all dis-eases in my life that is keeping me from receiving what you have for me at your table especially stubbornness, fear or pride that is causing me not to forgive. In Jesus name I have prayed".
Amen.

Then the speaker said *"If there is anyone here today that wants to receive Christ Jesus as their Lord and Savior come to me now while the Savior can be found."* This time it was Melody weeping because she watched Unique along with other women take the leap of faith to receive Christ. Next the speaker thanked everyone for having her then proceeded to give everyone one of her ministry cards. Melody wanted to know who was the women of God who spoke briefly but had an empowering effect on the women that day so she looked down at her card and it illustrated Sharon J. Thomas, Founder of Real Women Real Talk Outreach Ministry.

    Melody then walked up to Unique to embrace her and as they were embracing Unique felt a small child clinging to her leg. When she looked down it was Porsha. She immediately asked where did you come from and where is mommy? Porsha took her hand and there was her sister looking around for Porsha. Without thinking Unique embraced her sister and asked what are you doing here?

    She answered in a tear stained face "we have been living here since the day after your graduation. My ex told me he needed his space back because he made plans to move his new girlfriend in and it would be awkward if we were there. I did not call you because you were so angry with me, mom and dad I did not think you would care in spite of how we treated you".

Then Unique asked for forgiveness and stated she was in a very dark place of unforgiveness, pain along with anger at that time. Unique further explained she just did not know how to handle what she was going through. Also realizing she was not all the way there yet she took the leap of faith to start the process of being whole again. Unique asked her sister was she working and she stated ""yes and the shelter has a free daycare for those who work."

Then and there she told her sister that she had planned to get her own apartment with the money she saved but if we get one together, we could share the expenses. I am willing to put my own issues aside for the sake of Porsha and our well-being to live out the rest of our lives are you okay with that? Her sister replied "*yes* and I know Porsha would love that as well". At that point she brought them over to meet her friend Melody and put her sister's telephone number in her cellphone.

On the way home Unique shared her plans with Melody with a new found joy. Unique told Melody it did not feel right with her sister staying in a shelter with Porsha. Melody also asked Unique if it was ok to share the great news with her parents including her upcoming plans of reuniting with her sister by getting an apartment together. At the dinner table Melody's dad stated they would also love to gift Unique with furniture and food to get them started as a celebration toward her new beginning with her family. In addition, Melody's mom had added a request that Unique along with her family spend the holidays with them and allow them to pick them up for church.

Unique expressed how Melody's family always made her feel wanted, loved and never once showed any kind of discord about her being in their home. She concluded with streaming tears saying thank you all for making me feel significant by showing me what a family is supposed to look like. Then she turned to Melody…you have been a constant true friend and a shoulder to cry on with no reservations. I am going to take what I have learned from you to pour into the relationship with my sister and eventually with my mom. I have learned there are no perfect families, but as long as we keep God first, He will direct our path.

Immediately after Mary and Antionette finished praying in the chapel they returned to the waiting room floor near Cosandra's hospital room. After being there for a short while a nurse came over to let them know that Antionette was a perfect match for Cosandra. This struck up a conversation between the two women.

Mary explained to Antionette she believed her husband left her because she could not have his children although he never said anything. His behavior changed over the years and he became very distant once they were made aware of Mary's reason for not being able to conceive. His work schedule became very hectic and he was always having to work late. When I brought it up, he would simply state I am just trying to make a better life for us and promised he would start delegating his workload so he could be home more.

He did make good on his promise up until six months later he told me he received a promotion and would now have to travel out of town on some occasions to spearhead new acquisitions. I was not working and grew bored with just staying home alone. I would occasionally ask if I could accompany him on some of his out of town trips. At first, he stated it would be a great idea and then it abruptly stopped because his company told him it was not cost effective. So, I was back to spending a lot of time alone.

One night while we were having dinner, I asked him what did he think about adopting a baby. He stated they definitely could afford it and the sounds of little feet in our home would bring him great joy. After two years of waiting a baby girl was available for adoption and we named her Cosandra after his grandmother. I was so busy making a home for Cosandra I did not realize my husband was almost null and void at home, but I trusted my husband so I did not make a big deal about it because he was the bread winner. When he picked up and abandoned us without a word it devasted me as you know.

Just as Antionette was about to say something the hospital staff were returning Cosandra to her room for recovery. The doctor explained the surgery was completed successfully but Cosandra will remain in the hospital for one week and will need physical therapy. We have to keep Cosandra stress free, comfortable and maintain low blood pressures in efforts of her recovering fully.

At that moment, both Mary and Antionette looked at each other remembering what got her there in the first place. Once the doctor left Mary stated "Cosandra *was so angry when she ran out into traffic, I pray that she will wake up in peace as not to derail her recovery. I know it will be a long road to recovery after she leaves here and she will need an outlet to express herself so I think I am going to reach out to the founder of Real Women Real Talk Outreach Ministry proactively.*" Antionette followed up by saying "*I think that is a great idea for the sake of Cosandra which will allow her mind to be renewed. I would also like to make a suggestion that you find an outlet for yourself as well to bring harmony back into your household.*"

After a week-long task of trying to meet with Veronica alone unsuccessfully Hanna ran into Veronica at the grocery store. She asked Veronica *"would it be okay if we could meet outside."* Although Veronica was scared, she replied "yes ma'am." After they completed their individual grocery shopping the time had come for them to talk.

Hanna started out by saying to Veronica *"thank you so much for meeting with me and I know you and Johanna have been friends for a very long time that she considers you her sister. This meeting is in efforts of helping my daughter whom we both love so much."* Then she said *"do you know what happened to her and any idea who may have done this?"*

Veronica was a little reluctant but she also knew this day would come. She was very apologetic for her role and assured Hanna she did not know what happened to Johanna until last Sunday when Johanna told her. Hanna interjected and said *"I do not blame you Veronica or Johanna because my daughter made a choice to sneak out the house and go to a party as teenagers often do, but she did not deserve this."*

Veronica continued to tell Hanna what she saw at the party and who may have been involved. The minute Veronica was finished Hanna thanked Veronica for her help, gave her a long loving hug and they both retreated to their vehicles. Hanna felt relieved to know the whole story and as she drove home, she began to pray that God would bring it all together to obtain justice for his daughter Johanna.

Hanna decided that she would also call the detectives over her daughter's case. When she called, she was directed to Detective Johnson however, before she released what she had to offer she asked detective Johnson were there any new developments concerning her daughter's case. Detective Johnson explained there were no leads at this time. Afterwards she explained to the detective what she found out through a credible witness. He wrote down all of Hanna's information and said he would investigate it further then call her upon his findings.

Detective Johnson first interviewed with Veronica down at the police station to answer the questions of how, where and eventually who she allegedly thought was involved. As Veronica talked detective Johnson wrote it all down and as soon as she was done, she left. Next, he sought out Mike and Evan. When he got to Mike's home his mom answered the door, detective Johnson introduced himself, then he asked for Mike.

Mike's mom Carol said "I am his mother may I ask what do you need with my son"? Detective Johnson explained that her son may have some pertinent information on a case he was working and if he is not home right now can you ask him to come down to the station as he was handing her his card. Carol then asked "can I and my husband accompany him?" Detective Johnson informed her she and her husband were more than welcome to come. Detective Johnson then left to proceed to Evan's home.

Evan answered the door and Detective Johnson asked Evan would he be willing to come down to the station to answer some questions about a case he was working and Evan replied *"sure just let me inform my parents where I am going."* Immediately Evan's dad came to the door to probe further.

Detective Johnson of course explained and invited Mr. Wheeler to join them.

Evan was one-year shy of being eighteen so Mr. Wheeler sat in on the session with Detective Johnson. Johnson asked Evan a series of questions that would put Evan at the scene of the crime. Then he asked Evan if he knew Johanna and the look on his face told the detective he did. Detective Johnson then further explained that it was important that he tell the truthful events of that evening. Evan looked at his dad with tears in his eyes and said "I'm sorry dad", but his dad looked at him with perplexity.

Evan was scared but knew the day would come and even though it might cost him his freedom he wanted to be released from the torment of what he had done to Johanna. As he told the story of what happen his father jumped up and said "*no son we are getting a lawyer!*" On the other hand, Evan exclaimed "*no dad you taught me to own up to my wrong doings and I have been tormented every day because of what I did, so please sit down, please!*" As Mr. Wheeler slowly sat down in his chair Evan continued to tell the story of what happened in the room that evening at Mike's house including all who were involved.

Before detective Johnson took Evan into custody, he asked Evan if he would testify to the assault and name all parties concerned in the court of law. Evan replied *"yes."* Despite the fact Evan was being placed under arrest and placed in handcuffs Detective Johnson allowed Evan and his dad a brief moment together.

Whereas, detective Johnson utilized that time to request warrants for the arrest of the other four young men involved including a search warrant for Mike's room. One-by-one each of the three young men were arrested at their individual homes, proclaiming their innocence. It was not until they reached Mike's home that possibly ended the charade of their innocence when one of the officers found a pink cellphone under some clothes of Mike's bed where it was placed in a plastic evidence bag.

Straightaway Detective Johnson took the cellphone evidence, met with Johanna who was accompanied by her parents and showed her the phone. Johanna said *"that is my phone where did you find it?"* Johnson began to release the names and arrests which took place that day and stated "had it not been for Evan confessing and your parents strongly seeking the truth the case would still be ongoing."

Conversely, though we cannot release your cellphone to you right now because it is part of our evidence. Johanna, said "keep it I will just purchase another one." Instantly, detective Johnson asked "if you do not mind me asking how do you know these young men." Johanna came back with "I go to school with all of them and I remember turning each of them down toward their advances of me being their girlfriend." "To think they did this to me because I said no!"

Immediately after she began crying noticeably as her mom Hanna held her in her arms. Once detective Johnson left Johanna told her parents now that I know what happened to me and why I still need to find an exit for the agony I feel. Can I start Real Women Real Talk Outreach Ministry with the founder now…I am not ready for group sessions? Hanna replied *"yes of course I will give her a call."*

Lastly, Johanna expressed to her parents she know it was wrong for her to be disobedient to their instructions, daddy I especially understand why you are so hard on me being discerning of the people who operate outside of our household as well as our family teachings and as a result it will take time for you to trust me again. I began to understand during your search for answers on my behalf that this did not just happen to me it happened to you too. Please forgive me for putting you both through this, I am so sorry. They immediately embraced one another with tear stained faces.

Nurse Barbara entered Stacey's room at seven o'clock in the morning, awakened Brooklyn and Sheila to inform them Stacey was cleared for discharge. In addition, they would receive discharge papers detailing what steps were needed to further Stacey's recovery; with the understanding she would need to follow up with her primary doctor. Just as nurse Barbara was ending her sentence Stacey was starting to move around in her sleep and eventually woke up. When she opened her eyes, she saw her father and

Sheila standing close to her hospital bed. She then said "*I just cannot and struggle to believe Peaches is gone*".

Daddy her life was so much different from mine, but she always found the time to encourage me and others continually. When she explained to me how she lost her mom, her father never got over it and was being abused by her stepmom I clung to her because I did not have the same story. It is hard for me to understand how I am so loved in my household but there are many others around me who tell similar stories that of Peaches. I do not understand what would drive people to abuse their love ones and kill them without giving it a second thought.

Daddy I did not feel sorry for her however somehow, I felt every bit of her pain and I wanted to make it better but I do believe I made it bearable. Ms. Sheila how did her pain become my pain? Sheila responded and said "*I know that you and Peaches were close friends by the way you often talked about her. I believe most times when there is a strong bond or not between those, we come in contact with we develop a genuine sense of compassion. It was that very reason Christ so loved the world he gave his only begotten son (John 3:16 KJV)...he has an abundance of compassion for mankind."*

"Although we live in an era that Christ is not asking us to give up our children to show our love for him, he does require us to rejoice with them that do rejoice, and weep with them that weep (Romans 12:15 KJV). Keeping in mind that we must be careful not to confuse compassion for being in love. You see God has predestined assignments for each of us here on earth to complete and if we are not careful of his specific instructions, we can be led astray thus delaying the completion of our assignments. We can contribute this to being confused on whether God intended us to stay where we are for a short while or stay indefinitely."

"For example, most of your childhood was unfortunately without your biological mom and God brought me into your lives for the purpose of balance which meant he was setting me up to stay indefinitely for the sake of you. Why? Because he sees further than we can see and in efforts of preparing all of us for the right path."

"I would like to believe that Peaches stepmom was not always like who she portrayed to be and that she just got off the designated path for her life by allowing either her past or current issues to be her director. You see, if we do not seek Gods face daily, we too can fall victim to disorder in our minds, homes, lives and as we all know it undoubtedly did not work in her favor. I stand before you humbled in not speaking of God as though I know his ways one hundred percent because his ways are not our ways (Isaiah 55:8 KJV) and I have learned to trust in the Lord with all my heart and lean not onto my own understanding (Proverbs 3:5 KJV)."

"I can see in your watery eyes you really loved Peaches on whatever capacity you built…no judgement here, but it is time for you to learn the truth about your assignment in her life. So, I invite you to get to know him further with me by seeking the help we need as a family by consistently going to church in addition to you and I attending Real Women Real Talk Outreach Ministry sessions. Stacey replied *"mom and dad, I love you."*

Immediately after Brooklyn and Sheila left the room so Stacey could get dressed before nurse Barbara returned for Stacey's discharge. Sheila said *"she called me mom."* Brooklyn then turned to his wife and said *"thank you for saying yes and I thank God for placing you in our lives. I could not have done this without you."*

Macaela's parents tried very hard to bring Macaela out of the depression state of mind she was in but nothing seemed to work. Macaela stopped being active at school, shied away from spending time or conversations with her new found friends at school and just simply stayed in her room. Although Macaela agreed to try one-on-one sessions with the founder of Real Women Real Talk Outreach Ministry she repeatedly turned down her mom's invitations. Adaego was running out of ideas to help her daughter and then she remembered Adaku Macaela's long-time friend from Nigeria.

Adaego remembered how they were inseparable as little girls and they never seemed to get tired of one another. As a result, she wrote a letter to Adaku in hopes she could maybe by chance help bring her daughter back to her. This did not stop the daily and constant prayer that she conducted on behalf of her family.

Three weeks had passed and Adaego still had not heard from Adaku. Adaego started to think something has happened to them in Nigeria. Although Adaego was emotionally tired in trying to find closure for herself she knew she had to be strong and continue to believe that help was on the way. Adaego was starting to feel overwhelmed because she was still dealing with the death of her son which getting over was easier said than done. She knew it was a process and it was going to take some time.

Without thought, she dropped down to her knees and started to pray in an emotional plea to God. *I seek your face Father because this is all I know to do in times of trouble. We have been in trouble many times before but not like this.*

Not that I do not have faith in your reasoning it is the mere notion of losing my daughter also while my emotions try to take charge over me. I know you to be a God who will not hold that against me yet somehow you trust me to bring us as a family back to you in the midst of the storm. I know of no one who can take this tragedy to another level of good.

As I know you will continue to keep us in the wings of your arms, I say thank you for holding us close to your bosom. I confess to you I am getting weak so I invite you to take over and let your will be done. Amen.

Adaego got up from the floor, wiped her tears away and wearily started preparing dinner. She decided to make her husband and Macaela's favorite American dish, fried chicken, Spanish rice, blackeye peas and sweet tea. Before long it was time to sit down to eat with her family.

Idunnuola began the conversation at the table by asking everyone how was their day. Adaego said it was an overwhelming day for her because she could not find her way around the house to do the normal cleaning. However, after spending time with God she was given strength to prepare dinner.

Macaela then added that her day was too long and she could not wait to get home to her room. Idunnuola then explained the company he worked for was doing great and that next month everyone was going to receive a bonus for their hard work. Everyone then turned and looked at the empty chair that normally held Abdu as though they were waiting for him to speak of his day…but there was only silence.

The only words that were spoken after that were of Macaela who asked to be excused. She looked at her parents and went straight to her room. Macaela sobbed as she went upstairs and thought to herself why, Lord why. She laid across her bed and was awakened by a knock at the door. She said come in but remembered she locked the door to get undress and when she opened the door it was Adaku.

Immediately they embraced and cried together for hours because not only had they not seen each other in years but the circumstance was all too familiar. Adaku was the first one to start talking and she explained to Macaela that she understands first hand on how she feels. You and your family stopped by my home and encouraged us during the passing of my sibling. You did not hesitate to find help for me and my family. I am here to do the same for you.

Will you let me? Macaela answered in a low muttered voice I have so many unanswered concerns like how long will I keep reliving the day we were shot then awake in cold sweats, a part of me does not want to move forward in life in fear of slowly forgetting him, and I feel a sense of guilt because I survived yet I believe it was his voice of never-ending chatter that brought me out of the coma. I want to avenge my brother's death but I do not know where to begin or how to do it without going to jail. The men who did this still have not been caught.

Macaela, I do not think that Abdu would want you to give up on life and allow the cowards who killed him to get a free pass on living life to the fullest while his dreams and aspirations died with him. My sibling did not get to see what kind of life he would lead but God has been gracious to our family. I now have two sisters and one baby brother and I will gladly share any of them with you. I am confident you will love my baby brother although he cannot talk yet with understanding he always has a whole lot to say.

Besides my parents obtained visas and today is our first day in our new American home. Yes, girl I am here to stay and we are back together again. Therefore, you must get all the mental and emotional help you need so we can figure out a way to avenge our brother's death by making his voice count. I am optimistic something can be done legally because I do not want to waste all this fineness by going to jail. Immediately after they proceeded downstairs and while they were making their way Macaela asked Adaku how did you find me and Adaku said *"I received a letter from your mom."*

After Adaku and her family were served dinner the girls cleared the table and washed the dishes. Macaela was then introduced to Adaku's siblings. Before long it was time for Adaku and her family to leave for home. As soon as everyone was gone Macaela got her mother's attention then she asked her mom to set-up her first appointment with the founder of Real Women Real Talk Outreach Ministry.

The Purpose

Several positive flowing years had gone by before group sessions began where Unique, Cosandra, Johanna, Stacey and Macaela were included. However, there were some young ladies in the group who were meeting me for the very first-time verses having had a one-on-one session. At first everyone was a little apprehensive about sharing their individual names.

So, it began like this…good day everyone my name is Sharon J. Thomas founder of Real Women Real Talk Outreach Ministry. At this time, I would like everyone to take a prayer sheet and pass it down. Once everyone has received one, we will begin by reading it aloud then we will start our group session. I have been truly blessed by this prayer from a long-ago co-worker and I have been praying it ever since. Let us begin…The Sister Prayer:

Father, I ask you to bless my sister standing before you right now! Lord, show her a new revelation of your love and power. Holy Spirit, I ask you to minister to her spirit at this very moment. Where there is pain, give her your peace and mercy. Where there is doubting, release a renewed confidence in your ability to work through her.

Where there is tiredness, or exhaustion, I ask you to give her understanding, patience and strength as she learns submission to your leading. Where there is spiritual stagnation, I ask you to renew her by revealing your nearness, and by drawing her to greater intimacy with you. Where there is fear, reveal your love, and release to her your courage.

Where there is sin blocking her, reveal it, and break its hold over my sister's life. Bless her finances, give her greater vision, and raise her up as a leader, provide a friend to support, and encourage her. Give her discernment to recognize the demonic forces around her, and reveal to her the power you have in you to defeat it.

I ask you to do these things in the name of Jesus! Amen

Directly after going clockwise in a circle the participants were asked to state their first name. They were reluctant but followed the directive. Instantaneously though to break up the monotony in the room I decided to make a game out of it. So, I told them I would give fifty dollars to anyone who could name four people going clockwise in the circle directly after them, forty dollars to anyone who could name three and twenty dollars to anyone who could name two. That day I only lost twenty dollars but it was all worth it to see the women start a dialog among one another by saying how funny everyone looked trying to figure out each other's name.

After giving everyone a chance to settle down the history of how Real Women Real Talk Outreach Ministry was birthed was then explained. The ministry began as a woman's breakfast entitled Women Empowering Women one Saturday morning on Saturday, May 24, 2014, then elevated to a full service with breakfast on Saturday, May 23, 2015 where there was a mistress of ceremony, prayer, words of encouragement, a virtuous women skit, and an anointed praise dance. However, on September 24, 2016 God did a new thing by birthing Real Women Real Talk

Outreach Ministry only this time the ministry was called out of the regular brick and mortar buildings to visit women shelters in efforts of administering hope and encouragement utilizing the Word of God every other Sunday.

As a result, many women received from the table of Christ with a new mindset to do better for the sake of themselves and their children while some returned to their old habits. By July of 2017 one-on-one and group sessions were developed which is how we got where we are today. Many of you derived from our one-on-one sessions while some of you are here meeting the Real Women Real Talk Outreach Ministry for the first time. So today I invite you to become a part of a sanctified movement while you make an effort to find a better you, ways to be healed from past hurts, obtain new positive supporting friendships, self-control as well as how to seek help in the midst of life storms and above all eventually finding your individual life purpose.

This is where you make a conscious decision to either stay where you are in life or conquer the issues that is holding you back from being the woman you were designed to be. Real Women Real Talk Outreach Ministry is not a quick antidote for your issues but a proven direction to be strong in the Lord and in the power of His might (Ephesians 6:10-12 KJV). It is our belief that you are here because you want to change your individual situations by doing something instead of just idly sitting around while your issues are trying to snatch your God given lives away from you. We commend you all for taking the first steps of realizing you cannot do this on your own, isolation is not the key and it is better seeking help with a vengeance! Now, give yourselves a hand!

The room was full of excitement and it could be seen that most of the women were delighted to be there while a couple of them just sat with their arms crossed. The women were then asked to complete an anonymous index card stating their one-word issue(s). Suddenly one young lady stood up made an unannounced decision to leave the group by proceeding toward the exit. I asked the group to excuse me and I sought after her (Luke 15:1-7 NIV). It turned out she did not feel comfortable with declaring her issue in front of the group so a one-on-one session was established then she returned to her seat.

It was explained that people will not always be readily available for you to talk to as you are going through so today you are going to learn the first step to finding help in any reasonable given situation(s). The participants were then given a bible (KJV), we prayed for guidance, clear understanding on what to do and the obedience to follow through with what was being asked of them to do before they opened the Word of God. They were then directed to the concordance in back of the bible, and asked to look up the word anger also utilizing the table of contents to find the book needed. There were four scriptures presented (Psalms 103:8, Proverbs 15:1, Ephesians 4:31 and Col 3:21).

In that moment as each scripture was read it was discovered that when we demonstrate a burst of anger God is merciful and gracious in His dealings with us. However, the best way to handle a situation is to return a soft answer to avoid further rage into the situation, do not allow bitterness, evil speaking or spite be our key to handling the situation and that Fathers (parents) are required not to provoke their children to anger as not to discourage them. So, if you violated any of these you must return to the individual and apologize whether they accept it or not you have done your part.

On the other hand, if this has happened to you do not go to the individual and demand an apology you must let go and let God deal with them. Understand we do not need their apology to move us to the next level in God. The lesson here is not to let situations or people hold us captive by hindering our growth or keep us from the Father's table. We are better than that! In other words, the Lord gives us all free will, we must always use it wisely and according to His instructions in the bible. Remembering God is always the pilot and never a co-pilot.

Outside of that we will fail in life and be tossed back and forth in our mess or stress. Now, in saying that how many of us by a show of hands in this room today want to stay right where you are (there were no show of hands). Congratulations you just opened your door to a new beginning out of your own personal wilderness!

Prosperously, the Real Women Real Talk Outreach Ministry group meetings continued every other week as scheduled. Majority of the women continued in the Real

Women Real Talk Outreach Ministry sessions for two years. During one session one participant asked how did I become so passionate and knowledgeable about what to do in times of trouble. I answered "*I began to know him for myself*".

At twelve I spent most of my time hanging with my brother and his friends because I was not into boys like the girls in my neighborhood. As result, I became a tom boy for four years (age 12 to 15). I further explained that I also grew up thinking I was adopted until the age of sixteen because there were pictures of my siblings but none of me. When I asked why while trying to complete a family tree school project where we had to add a baby picture, I was told I was ugly so no pictures were taken. This coming from a parent was very painful.

But something inside of me would not let me give up at that time. I was constantly verbally and physically abused by both parents, told I would never amount to anything, the prostitute of the block because they assumed I was sleeping with the guys I was hanging out with, and was always wrong when it came to any wrongful issues that developed in our household no matter if I said I did not do it. At seventeen I just could not take it anymore and acted out a failed attempt of ending my life. At eighteen I fell in love with my high school sweet heart, and he asked me to marry him before he was to go off to the military.

    My family was very dysfunctional including domestic abuse by my father towards my mom. There was no one to talk to because we were told never air our dirty laundry (keep our family business to ourselves). The domestic violence continued until my mom got tired of it and left us with our father because she could not afford to take us with her according to the meeting, she had with us before she left. I felt the only love I had to hang onto was my fiancé but that was quickly distinguished when I found him in bed with a relative. Being devasted by my life issues I withdrew from everything and became shutoff from the world.

    I then fell for a young man who pursued and showed a real interest in me. However, after two years when things did not work according to his plan, he became abusive and because my childhood did not show me anything different, I endured his abuse right down to the day he assaulted me. I started to believe this was what love was supposed to be and if I left him, I would have no one to love me. Until one day I got tired of abuse coming from him as well as my father I called my mom who already took in my older sister and asked if I could stay with her. After a dead silence of about five-minutes or so waiting for her answer she finally said yes, but by the time she answered tears were already streaming down my face because I felt no one wanted me.

    My mom eventually moved into a larger apartment to house me and my sister but the treatment towards me did not change. At eighteen I moved into my own apartment. At twenty I was invited to a church down the block from my apartment. I decided to go and found It was not a typical church of my culture…it was a Hispanic church that opened their arms to me with no hesitation. Pastor Rodriquez had his daughter sit next to me for translation purposes.

    Once prayer began, I was immediately hit with the Holy Spirit. At first, I was scared because I did not know if something was wrong with me then I was told by Pastor Rodriquez to let God have his way with me. It did not hurt so I did and it felt like I was being emptied which is how I can best describe it. I grew to love the leadership and church members and the way they always made me feel welcomed. I eventually joined the church and three weeks later I was baptized. After the baptism they held a fellowship brunch in my honor at our church. I of course was very emotional because I had never been celebrated before…not even a birthday party that I could remember.

    I stayed with the church for about two and a half years because my old abusive boyfriend reared his ugly head and showed up at the new apartment. Only this time I called the police however they would always show up hours after he had done his damage and gone. It was not until I started praying that doors started to open for me. I asked God to please remove me from this situation and by faith I packed my things as though he had already done it. Three weeks later I was a resident of Dekalb County in Atlanta, Georgia.

    I left behind a great promising job from the Trade Center (Twin Towers) to Wall Street but I did not care I wanted out of despair. I told my family prior to me leaving that I was exiting New York, but I did not feel safe telling them where I was going especially after observing my father from afar giving my abusive ex-boyfriend money so, I kept my whereabouts to myself. It is a good thing too because I later found out my ex-boyfriend was told I moved to Florida because I visited their two times. Not to mention the devastation that took place on September 11, 2001 when a plane went through the Trade Centers killing a multitude of first responders and I knew first-hand what it took to get out of the buildings.

So, you see you are not alone in your individual temporary anguish Christ sent people like me who could identify with what you have gone or currently going through. Now, you know I am not here because I heard God is good, I am here because I experienced Christ Jesus for myself. At one point I could not share what I endured but God has given me a bold voice of transparency to help all of you and others to come to realize our set backs are a set up for God to show anyone coming against us who we working with!

After a year or so I got to see God shine through Unique, Cosandra, Johanna, Stacey and Macaela. Unique ultimately reunited with her mom at her established apartment and found her passion through helping others with their anger management by way of her church affiliate. Both Cosandra and Johanna joined a church to strengthen their individual walk with Christ, by helping youths with abandonment and sexual assault matters. Stacey turned her life over to Christ with the assistance of her stepmom Sheila, became a blossoming woman of God and helped abused youths in honor of Peaches. Whereas Macaela and Adaku helped neighborhoods understand the importance of neighborhood watch programs within and outside of their individual neighborhoods to avoid what happened to Macaela naming themselves Abdu's Watchful Eye Foundation. Equally they all received their individual healing by helping others find peace in the midst of their life storms and by compelling others to come to Christ (Luke 14:23 KJV) which is our ultimate life purpose.

God gives us all the opportunity to place our burdens upon Him, and he shall sustain us; he shall never suffer the righteous to be moved (Psalms 55:22 KJV). Conversely, we have the victory so why are we trying to hold unto something or someone if they mean us no good. He made us more than conquers (Romans 8:37 KJV). What do we have to lose by trusting in Him who made us? Nothing. Do you know most of the time it is our natural fears or pride that is keeping us from our true purpose destination in life? *"The Holy Spirit says, today if you will hear his voice, harden not your hearts out of rebellion, as in the day of temptation in the wilderness (Hebrews 3:7-8 KJV)".*

    I say to you fear not for he is with us, do not let discouragement be your guide let him in to be your Lord. If you need strength let him in because he will be the advocate for you with the right hand of His righteousness (Isaiah 41:10 KJV). Do not be afraid to talk to him regarding your concerns just take your petition in prayer to him with thanksgiving letting your request be known unto God. In efforts of receiving a kind of peace that passes all understanding through Jesus Christ (Philippians 4:6-7 KJV). Of course, you will have other situations or people come into your path trying to distract you from your true destiny…only this time you have the right ammunition to endure!

God's door is always open so come out of your dark places into the light and stop letting people or situations direct your path. Speak it and treat it or them like a drug and say no! *No, you cannot have my mind, family, children, siblings, finances, house, car, health, sight, life or church! No, you cannot take the place of what God has for me…I said NO! I say this with the true authority that has been empowered within me and I demand you to return to the dark hole you slithered out of in the name of Jesus!*

Be advised though, you "will not" be able to demand anything from the gates of hell until you give your life to Christ to be reborn again, believe in his death, burial and resurrection. Look at it in terms of how can the Father truly protect you if you are operating outside His Word of instructions. His terms are somewhat similar to the laws of this world…the law-abiding police cannot keep you out of jail or away from the death penalty if you refuse to obey the law. Moving forward in life requires work from us like praying without ceasing as Apostle Paul instructs us to do (1 Thessalonians 5:17 KJV) and putting on the full armor of God (Ephesians 6:10-18 KJV).

What I have also learned is that we will always have challenges in life but the difference is when we lay our concerns at the feet of Jesus, we will receive peace beyond our own understanding because God has already overcome the world (John 16:33 KJV). No one is able or can speak boldly in taking on the concerns of the entire world and get up with all power except him! Do not be dismayed if it feels like you have more challenges than most people it just simply means now that you are walking in righteousness the enemy is trying to get you to return to your former ways before you gave your life to Christ. Instead of telling your God about your issues try telling your issues about the God you serve!

Speaking from experience I could not have done any of this on my own I desperately needed God to take the wheel and be my pilot. I am here to say the journey was not easy considering we live in a world that does not like to wait. Once we turn our lives over to Christ, we start to believe blessings will come to us like we put food in a microwave and wait for the ding. This is not how God operates it is according to his timing, preparation and our maturity. I encourage you to observe the lives of others who profess Christ, encamp yourself around those who truly walk in his principles inside as well as outside the church, pray to God which church he wants you to attend and/or be a member, be pliable to the instructions of Christ, never be afraid to ask for help and He will direct your path.

I remember as a babe in Christ I was given instructions while sitting in church to give my last fifty dollars to an unknown woman sitting next to me. Of course, I hesitated in thinking because I was concerned about how was I going to feed my family for the rest of the month. However, after service was over, I followed the directive, the woman starting crying and saying this was truly an answer to her prayers that day because she lost her job with the inability to feed her children. As I was making my way home, I thanked God for using me in a way that I had never been used before and not long after I got home there was a knock at the door. It was my sister who was under the influence of drugs (crack) with three bags of groceries.

I offered her to come in to eat with us but she refused saying she had somewhere else to be. I cried after she left because I knew without a doubt it was God who sent her on my behalf because as we all know a person under the influence of crack cocaine concerns is primarily getting their next fix. That day I learned that God can use anyone to bless us in times of uncertainty when we are obedient and trust his specific instructions.

So, today I invite you to embrace what God has to offer and do not look back! Today and every day that I have breath in my body I declare and decree that if He did it for them, "if He did it for me"…He will do the same for you.

Reflection Questions

1. Did you identify with any of the life changing scenarios? What did you get out of it?

2. What part of the book blessed you the most? How do you feel about it?

3. Which one of the life issues fed your spirit to be compelled to do something different outside of what you regularly do?

4. What immediate change took place after you finished reading the book? Will you continue on your changed path per the instructions given for a better future?

5. Based on who you know do you think they would benefit from receiving the same blessing that changed your life? What would you do to make sure they did?

Words from the author

I would like to thank you for blessing the ministry by making a purchase. We recognize that you did not have to but you did it anyhow. Our prayers are that you grow strong into your reborn lifestyle remembering nothing happens overnight, it is a process that will happen over the course of your life.

But you, Lord, are a shield around me, my glory, the One who lifts my head high I call out to the Lord, and he answers me from his holy mountain. I lie down and sleep; I wake again, because the Lord sustains me. (Psalms 3:5 NIV).

Thank you, Lord, for making all of this possible.

In His Service,

Sharon J. Thomas

Outreach Ministry

We encourage your feedback about your book experience:

sthomas@realwomentalk.net

Made in the USA
Columbia, SC
11 July 2023